CHICKEN
NIGHT

KATE McMILLAN

PHOTOGRAPHS BY ERIN KUNKEL

weldon**owen**

CONTENTS

CHICKEN FOR DINNER

For most people, a chicken dish is a familiar and welcome sight on the dinner table, whether it is a weeknight family supper, a casual get-together with friends, or an elegant meal for special guests. But that remarkable versatility is just one reason why chicken is so popular. Chicken is great, too, because it lends itself to different cooking techniques and seasonings, is a good source of low-fat meat protein, and is easy to cook, making it an excellent choice for cooks with busy lifestyles.

In these pages, you'll discover more than 50 chicken recipes organized by cooking method. In summer, you might turn to the grill chapter for chicken teriyaki or chicken skewers; in winter, oven-cooked chicken with corn-bread stuffing or tandoori chicken wings might appeal; and year-round, stove-top options such as a stir-fry, a curry, or a sauté are ideal. A chapter of comfort-food classics includes such favorites as fried chicken, chicken enchiladas, and a potpie. This focus on variety extends to the cuts used as well, with thighs and drumsticks, breasts and wings, and whole birds all featured.

You'll also find a chapter on easy-to-make salads and sides, from a mix of fennel, apple, and radish to roasted potatoes and coconut-laced jasmine rice, to complement whichever chicken dish you choose. Plus, you'll learn how to cut up a whole bird into serving pieces, choose the best cut and season for any dish, and plan menus for every occasion.

A chicken dinner is all about variety, whether it's drumettes or drumsticks for the kids, lean breast meat for the calorie conscious, a whole roast bird for the traditionalist, or a Thai curry for the adventurous. But it's also about how easy it can be to put together a chicken dinner, so that the cook enjoys the meal just as much as everyone else at the table.

ANATOMY OF A CHICKEN DISH

A whole chicken includes both white meat—breasts and wings—and dark meat—drumsticks and thighs. Different cuts are better suited for certain preparations. Here's a guide on how to select the best cut for cooking.

WHOLE CHICKEN

Roasting or grilling a whole chicken is one of the easiest, hands-off ways to put a delicious dinner on the table. Buying a whole chicken is also your most economical option. You can cook and serve it whole, or you can divide up the cooked bird and use the meat in salads, sandwiches, soup, or other dishes. Or, you can cut up the raw chicken and use the various cuts for different recipes.

CARVING A WHOLE COOKED CHICKEN

To carve the chicken into serving pieces, place it breast side up on a carving board with a groove around the perimeter to collect the juices. Pull on a wing to locate the joint that connects it to the body, then, using a large, sharp knife, cut through the joint. Repeat with the other wing and transfer the wings to a serving platter. Next, move a drumstick to find the hip joint, then remove the whole leg (drumstick and thigh) by cutting through the joint. Separate the thigh and drumstick by cutting through the joint that connects the two and transfer both pieces to the platter. Repeat with the other leg. Now, stand the chicken upright on the board and, using a large, heavy knife, cut straight down through the middle of the bird to remove the back. You can use the back to make stock or you can discard frame after you have picked the meat off of it. Next, cut straight down the breast plate to separate the breasts into 2 pieces. Finally, cut each breast half crosswise into 2 pieces and transfer the pieces to the serving platter. You should have 10 pieces total, 4 breast pieces, 2 drumsticks, 2 thighs, and 2 wings.

WINGS

Although some cooks send the wings to the stockpot, they are also great fried, broiled, or baked. Or, you can use just the drumette, the upper, meaty part of the wing, which, like the wing itself, makes great finger food.

DRUMSTICKS

Championed as classic "game-day food," drumsticks are often fried or baked with a spicy or sticky sauce. That's because a relatively small amount of meat surrounds the bone and thick or gooey sauce helps keep the meat tender throughout the cooking process. Plus, the shape of the drumstick makes it perfect finger food–easy to grasp, or even dip into a sauce, without a utensil.

BREASTS

Arguably the most versatile cut, and a great source of low-fat protein, the breast provides the most meat. A little goes a long way, making it a good choice for roasting then shredding for filling sandwiches, for stuffing enchiladas, or for mixing into salads and pastas. It can also be quickly grilled or sautéed and served when it is just done and still succulent. To save time, cook several breasts at once to use throughout the week (cooked chicken will keep in the refrigerator for up to 5 days).

THIGHS

The darker meat of thighs also carries more fat, which means its preparation requires less added fat. Naturally juicy and flavorful, thighs adapt to almost any method–stove top, grill, and oven. They are also the perfect size for a single serving.

CHICKEN PRIMER

Making chicken needn't be boring or labor-intensive, especially if you start with fresh, great-quality poultry and follow a few basic tips for cooking and seasoning. With just a few tools, a little prep, and a great recipe, you'll be able to turn out tempting chicken dishes throughout the week for simple suppers and get-togethers.

PICK A CUT Use the chicken cut called for in the recipe or select the cut best suited to your chosen cooking method (see page 9). If serving a group, consider buying a mix of cuts, or a whole chicken, so each person can pick his or her favorite piece.

SELECT THE BEST Most of the recipes in this book feature chicken combined with just a handful of other ingredients. For the tastiest results, seek out locally raised, free-range birds, preferably organic, and the freshest, best-quality ingredients you can afford.

ORGANIZE PREP Dishes come together easily when the ingredients and tools are laid out before you start to cook. Prep and measure the chicken and other ingredients, keeping each ingredient in its own bowl or container. Some dishes can be assembled and then frozen, ready to be thawed and placed in the oven on busy weeknights.

PRACTICE CHICKEN SAFETY Be aware of cross-contamination when working with raw chicken. Use hot water and soap to clean any cutting board or knife that comes into contact, and make sure neither the chicken nor the tools come into contact with other surfaces or ingredients. Wash your hands well while working. A clean, empty sink is a good place to keep the bird until you're ready to cook. Always cook chicken to 165°F (74°C).

PAT IT DRY Always pat a whole chicken dry with paper towels before roasting or grilling. Any dampness will create steam, making a crispy skin impossible.

SEASON BOLDLY Chicken takes well to robust seasoning. Start with a generous sprinkle of salt and pepper, add the herbs and spices listed in the recipe, and then embellish with more herbs—especially fresh herbs—if you like.

MAINTAIN FLAVOR To avoid meat that is dry and tasteless, never underseason or overcook chicken. Marinating chicken for up to 24 hours before cooking will help lock in moisture and flavor and works especially well for recipes that call for baking, roasting, or grilling. You can also heighten flavor by topping the chicken with a quick pan sauce made from garlic, wine, stock, and your favorite herbs and spices.

SERVE PROMPTLY Chicken tastes best served the day it's cooked, ideally while still hot and juicy. Allow grilled and baked dishes to cool for 5–10 minutes, then serve right away. Although sauced and fried dishes fade after a day in the refrigerator, cooked chicken meat from any dish can be shredded and used for salads, pastas, and sandwiches.

TOOLS FOR SUCCESS

These simple tools will help you create amazing chicken dishes every time.

GRILL PAN & OUTDOOR GRILL
An outdoor grill imparts a wonderful smoky flavor to chicken, and a stove-top grill pan is a great solution for the cooler months.

PLASTIC CUTTING BOARD
A dishwasher-friendly plastic cutting board can be washed more easily and thoroughly than a wooden cutting board.

SHARP KNIVES Cutting chicken, boneless or not, requires sharp knives. Keep a variety of different-size knives on hand for paring off fat, removing skin, and cutting up whole chickens.

WOODEN SPOON Many chicken dishes benefit from a quick pan sauce, which begins with scraping up the brown bits left behind in a pan. A wooden spoon or flat wooden spatula will help with this task without damaging the pan.

ROASTING & SAUTÉ PANS A good-quality roasting pan and a sauté pan will handle dozens of recipes.

BRINGING IT ALL TOGETHER

Here are ways to make chicken for dinner
easy on the cook and fun for everyone.

MAKING IT A MEAL

A simple side dish or two will turn almost any
chicken dish into a full meal.

STIR-FRIES Add steamed brown or white rice.

BAKED DISHES Add sliced or cubed vegetables
and/or potatoes to the baking dish for a one-pot
supper; serve with a green salad.

WINGS Add crudités with a dipping sauce
or accompany with a salad of chopped and/or
shredded raw vegetables.

SAUCED DISHES Add sliced nuts, chopped dried fruits,
or fresh herbs for additional flavor and nutrition.

GRILLED DISHES Grill corn, asparagus, sliced
vegetables (such as zucchini, bell peppers,
or eggplant), or vegetable kebabs alongside
the chicken.

SHORTCUTS FOR A BUSY DAY

Here are a few tips to help get dinner on the
table quickly when your schedule is tight.

READY-TO-GO CHICKEN Ask your butcher to cut the chicken
into the exact-size pieces you need and to remove any
unwanted fat or skin. For added ease, pick up a rotisserie
chicken to use in recipes like panini or enchiladas.

FRONT LOAD PREP Get a head start in the beginning of the
week by washing lettuces, chopping vegetables, or making
sauces or dressings to store in the refrigerator.

PREPARED ITEMS Purchase pesto or other jarred sauces
for easy assembly. Or, pick up a favorite premade salad or
vegetable dish from the deli counter to round out the meal.

ENTERTAINING TIPS

Whether inviting friends over for a casual weeknight supper or hosting a weekend barbecue, chicken is a great and versatile choice for feeding a crowd. Here are some ideas for dinner parties.

STIR-FRY PARTY Place chopped or sliced fresh vegetables, garlic, ginger, and green onions in separate bowls alongside a bowl of ground or cubed, skinless chicken. Set out a row of condiments, such as soy sauce, fish sauce, and chile sauce, and then heat up a wok—or two woks, if possible. Invite your guests to customize their stir-fries from the buffet of ingredients and cook up individual servings in the wok. Round out the menu with a pot of steamed rice and lettuce cups for scooping.

GRILL PARTY Pick a couple crowd-friendly recipes, such as Beer Can Chicken (page 73) or a couple of skewered dishes. Throw some fresh vegetables, lightly coated in oil, on the grill to cook alongside the chicken, then grill stone fruits or other fruits for dessert and serve over vanilla ice cream or with fresh whipped cream. Ask your guests to bring their favorite beverages and a simple green salad to bring it all together.

ONE-POT PARTY Baked dishes are ideal for feeding a crowd. Add some sliced or cubed vegetables and/or potatoes to the baking dish and the dinner is nearly done. Because the main dish requires no attention once it is in the oven, you'll have time to make a special side dish, such as Shaved Fennel, Radish & Apple Salad (page 110).

WINGS & DRUMSTICKS PARTY Prepare a platter of drumsticks and wings, two great finger foods. Add some crudités with a couple of dipping sauces, a warm loaf of rustic bread, and plenty of napkins and ice cold beer.

FRIED CHICKEN PARTY Make batches of this quick-cooking favorite to feed a crowd. Serve with classic accompaniments, such as a skillet corn bread, Buttermilk Mashed Potatoes (page 116), and corn on the cob.

CHICKEN

stovetop • oven • grill • classics

3 boneless, skinless chicken breasts, about 1½ lb (750 g) total

½ cup (2½ oz/75 g) all-purpose flour

Kosher salt and freshly ground pepper

3 tablespoons olive oil

2 tablespoons unsalted butter, at room temperature

2 cloves garlic, chopped

1 jar (6 oz/185 g) artichoke hearts, rinsed, drained, and quartered

1 cup (8 fl oz/250 ml) dry white wine

½ cup (4 fl oz/125 ml) low-sodium chicken broth

Juice of 1 lemon

2 tablespoons capers, rinsed and drained

1 tablespoon chopped fresh parsley

CHICKEN PICCATA WITH ARTICHOKES

Cut each chicken breast in half through the thickness (as if you were going to open it like a book, but cut all the way through). Working with 1 half at a time, place the chicken between 2 pieces of plastic wrap and pound with the flat side of a meat pounder or other flat-topped heavy metal object to a thickness of about ¼ inch (6 mm).

Pour the flour onto a large plate and season it well with salt and pepper. Dredge the chicken in the seasoned flour, shaking off the excess. Warm 2 tablespoons of the olive oil in a large frying pan over medium-high heat until very hot but not smoking. Working in batches as needed to avoid crowding, add the chicken and cook, turning once, until golden brown on both sides and opaque throughout, about 4 minutes per side. Transfer to a plate and set aside.

Return the frying pan to medium-high heat; do not wipe the pan clean. Melt 1 tablespoon of the butter in the remaining 1 tablespoon olive oil. Add the garlic and artichoke hearts and sauté just until the garlic is soft, about 1 minute. Stir in the wine, scraping up any browned bits on the bottom of the pan. Bring to a simmer and cook until the liquid reduces by about half, about 3 minutes. Stir in the broth, lemon juice, and capers. Reduce the heat to medium, bring to a gentle simmer, and whisk in the remaining 1 tablespoon butter. Cook, stirring occasionally, until the sauce thickens slightly, about 5 minutes longer. Stir in the parsley. Taste and adjust the seasoning.

Return the chicken to the pan and turn to coat each piece with the sauce. Cook just until the chicken is warmed through, about 2 minutes. Serve right away.

SERVES 6

A HEALTHY TWIST

Piccata refers to a type of Italian dish where thin pieces of meat are coated in flour and sautéed in butter and oil. This updated version is made with savory artichoke hearts. For extra vegetables, add a few handfuls of fresh spinach along with the capers. Serve this dish over a plate of orzo or other small pasta shape for soaking up the delicious sauce.

WHAT YOU NEED

2 cups (16 fl oz/500 ml) low-sodium chicken broth

1 teaspoon saffron threads

1 tablespoon olive oil

6 bone-in, skin-on chicken thighs, about 2½ lb (1.25 kg) total

Kosher salt and freshly ground pepper

8 oz (250 g) chorizo, sliced

½ yellow onion, chopped

4 cloves garlic, minced

1½ teaspoons smoked paprika

1 can (14½ oz/455 g) chopped tomatoes

1 cup (7 oz/220 g) short-grain rice

½ cup (2½ oz/75 g) frozen peas

2 tablespoons chopped fresh parsley

CHICKEN PAELLA

MIX IT UP

→→→→→→→→

With fragrant saffron rice as the base, nearly any combination of vegetables and protein is delicious here. Quartered artichokes, chopped asparagus, roasted red pepper strips, and sweet Italian sausage pieces are also tasty. All this one-pot meal needs is a glass of red wine or sparkling cranberry juice, and dinner is served.

Warm the broth in a saucepan over medium heat. Add the saffron threads, stirring to help dissolve. Reduce the heat to very low and cover to keep warm.

Warm the olive oil in a paella pan or a large, heavy-bottomed sauté pan over medium-high heat. Season the chicken all over with salt and pepper. Working in batches as needed to avoid crowding, add the chicken to the hot pan, skin side down, and cook, turning once, until golden brown on both sides, about 4 minutes per side. Transfer to a plate and set aside.

Add the chorizo to the pan, still over medium-high heat, and cook, tossing and stirring, until browned on both sides, about 3 minutes total. Add the onion and sauté until soft, about 3 minutes. Stir in the garlic and paprika and cook just until the garlic is soft, about 30 seconds. Stir in the tomatoes with their juices, scraping up any browned bits on the bottom of the pan. Stir in the rice and the warm saffron broth. Season well with salt and pepper and bring to a boil. Fold in the peas, then return the chicken to the pan, nestling it in the sauce. Reduce the heat to medium-low, cover, and cook until the rice is tender and the chicken is opaque throughout (no pink should show when you cut in next to a bone, and the chicken juices should run clear), about 20 minutes.

Remove from the heat and let the paella rest, covered, for 10 minutes. Stir in the parsley. Taste and adjust the seasoning. Serve right away.

SERVES 4–6

3 tablespoons hoisin sauce	3 tablespoons Asian fish sauce
1 tablespoon rice vinegar	2 tablespoons low-sodium soy sauce
½ teaspoon hot pepper sauce such as Sriracha (optional)	2 tablespoons fresh lemon juice
2 tablespoons peanut or canola oil	⅓ cup (½ oz/15 g) loosely packed fresh cilantro leaves, chopped
2 cloves garlic	3 tablespoons pine nuts, toasted
¼–½ teaspoon red pepper flakes	1 head romaine or iceberg lettuce
1½ lb (750 g) ground chicken	

CHICKEN IN LETTUCE CUPS

To make the sauce, in a small bowl, whisk together the hoisin, vinegar, and hot sauce, if using. Set aside.

Warm the oil in a large frying pan over medium-high heat. Add the garlic and red pepper flakes and sauté just until the garlic is soft, about 1 minute. Add the chicken and cook, stirring occasionally and using your spoon to break up any clumps, until the meat is cooked through, 5–8 minutes.

Stir in the fish sauce, soy sauce, and lemon juice. Remove from the heat and stir in the cilantro and pine nuts.

To assemble, core and separate the lettuce head into individual leaves, using only the sturdy, cup-shaped leaves; reserve the flimsy or flat leaves for another use. Arrange 1 or 2 of the lettuce "cups" on each of 4 plates, or arrange smaller lettuce leaves on a platter for appetizers. Spoon the chicken mixture into each leaf. Drizzle with the sauce and serve right away.

SERVES 4

ADD SOME CRUNCH

To add even more crunch to this recipe, top the chicken with grated carrots, sliced water chestnuts or radishes, or red pepper strips on top of the chicken. Serve this light dinner alongside sesame noodles or steamed, frozen dumplings. For a fun party appetizer, serve the chicken mixture in endive boats.

3 tablespoons olive oil

6 boneless, skinless chicken thighs, about 2 lb (1 kg) total

Kosher salt and freshly ground pepper

3 tablespoons chopped shallots

¾ cup (6 fl oz/180 ml) dry white wine

⅔ cup (5 fl oz/160 ml) low-sodium chicken broth

6 tablespoons (3 fl oz/90 ml) heavy cream

3 tablespoons Dijon mustard

2 tablespoons chopped fresh tarragon

SAUTÉED CHICKEN WITH MUSTARD-TARRAGON CREAM SAUCE

SAUTÉING MASTER

The most important rule in mastering the art of sautéing is to never crowd the pan. Take the time to sauté your food in batches so that it cooks evenly and caramelizes beautifully. Serve this chicken with brown or white rice mixed with chopped fresh parsley and Shaved Fennel, Radish & Apple Salad (page 110).

Warm 2 tablespoons of the olive oil in a large frying pan over medium-high heat. Season the chicken all over with salt and pepper and add to the pan. Cook, turning once, until golden brown on both sides and opaque throughout, about 6 minutes per side. Transfer the chicken to a plate and pour off the fat from the pan; do not wipe the pan clean.

Return the frying pan to medium-high heat. Warm the remaining 1 tablespoon olive oil in the hot pan. Add the shallots and sauté just until soft, about 2 minutes. Stir in the wine, scraping up any browned bits on the bottom of the pan. Bring to a simmer and cook until the liquid reduces by about half, about 3 minutes. Whisk in the broth, cream, and mustard, reduce the heat to medium, and bring to a gentle simmer. Cook, stirring occasionally, until the sauce thickens, about 4 minutes longer. Stir in the tarragon and season with salt and pepper.

Return the chicken to the pan and toss it in the sauce to coat well. Cook just until the chicken is warmed through. Using tongs, transfer the chicken to a serving platter and spoon the sauce over the top. Serve right away.

SERVES 4–6

Kosher salt and freshly ground pepper

¾ lb (375 g) broccoli, trimmed and cut into small florets

2 tablespoons low-sodium soy sauce

2 teaspoons rice vinegar

1 teaspoon cornstarch

1 lb (500 g) boneless, skinless chicken breasts, cut into ½-inch (12-mm) cubes

¼ cup (2 fl oz/60 ml) low-sodium chicken broth

2 tablespoons oyster sauce

2 teaspoons sherry

2 tablespoons peeled and minced fresh ginger

2 cloves garlic, minced

3 tablespoons cashews

Hot pepper sauce for serving (optional)

CHICKEN, BROCCOLI & CASHEW STIR-FRY

Bring a saucepan of salted water to a boil over high heat. Add the broccoli and cook until tender-crisp, about 3 minutes. Drain well and set aside.

In a large bowl, whisk together 1 tablespoon of the soy sauce, the vinegar, and ½ teaspoon of the cornstarch. Season with salt and pepper and add the chicken. Toss the chicken in the marinade and let stand at room temperature for 10 minutes.

In a small bowl, whisk together the broth, oyster sauce, sherry, the remaining 1 tablespoon soy sauce, and the remaining ½ teaspoon cornstarch. Set aside.

Warm a wok or a large, nonstick frying pan over high heat. When the pan is very hot, add the chicken and all of its marinade and toss and stir until the chicken is opaque throughout, about 6 minutes. Stir in the ginger and garlic and cook just until the aromatics are soft and fragrant, about 30 seconds.

Stir in the oyster sauce mixture and let simmer, stirring once or twice, until the sauce thickens, about 2 minutes. Stir in the cashews and broccoli and serve right away. Pass the hot sauce at the table, if using.

SERVES 4–6

QUICK DISH

Stir-fries are a perfect weeknight dinner solution, as they cook quickly and are versatile. For a meal that comes together in minutes, have all the ingredients prepped and ready to go and make sure your pan is very hot before you start cooking. To check if your pan is hot enough, toss a drop of water into it; if it sizzles, it's ready. Serve this dish with steamed rice.

1 lb (500 g) boneless, skinless chicken thighs or breasts

1 tablespoon olive oil

Kosher salt and freshly ground pepper

4 slices thick-cut bacon

2 cloves garlic, minced

4 green onions, white and tender green parts only, chopped

3 tablespoons oyster sauce

2 tablespoons low-sodium soy sauce

6 cups (30 oz/940 g) cooked long-grain rice (about 2 cups/14 oz/440 g uncooked), cooled

½ cup (2½ oz/75 g) fresh shelled or thawed frozen peas

½ cup (2½ oz/75 g) thawed frozen carrots

3 large eggs, beaten

CHICKEN FRIED RICE

ASIAN NIGHT

This delicious Chinese rice dish is a great way to use up leftover rice. Make a double batch of rice for one meal, then cover and refrigerate the cooled leftovers. The colder the grains, the better, as it helps create an extra-crispy dish. For a fast Asian-themed meal, serve fried rice with Sesame Sugar Snap Peas (page 109). In a pinch, use leftover cooked chicken or the meat from a store-bought rotisserie chicken.

Preheat the oven to 375°F (190°C).

Place the chicken on a baking sheet. Drizzle with the olive oil, season well with salt and pepper, and toss to coat. Bake, turning once about halfway through, until opaque throughout, about 25 minutes. Remove from the oven and let cool. When the chicken is cool enough to handle, cut into small dice and set aside.

While the chicken is baking, in a wok or a large, nonstick frying pan over medium-high heat, fry the bacon until crispy, about 6 minutes. Transfer to paper towels to drain. When the bacon is cool enough to handle, tear it into bite-sized pieces. Set aside.

Pour off all but 1 tablespoon of the fat in the pan and place the pan over high heat. When the fat is hot, add the garlic and green onions and cook, stirring constantly, just until the garlic softens, about 30 seconds. Add the oyster sauce and soy sauce and stir to combine well. Add the rice and fold, toss, and stir until it is completely covered in the sauce. Fold in the peas, carrots, chicken, and bacon and cook, stirring once or twice gently, until warmed through, about 3 minutes.

Push the rice mixture to one side of the pan and add the eggs to the other. Let them cook for about 20 seconds before you start to scramble them with a rubber spatula. When the eggs are softly cooked, break them into pieces and fold them into the rice. When the eggs are all cooked and everything is nicely incorporated, season with salt and pepper and serve right away.

SERVES 4–6

Kosher salt and freshly ground pepper

1 lb (500 g) sweet potatoes

2 tablespoons canola oil, plus more as needed

1 lb (500 g) boneless, skinless chicken thighs

1 yellow onion, cut into 8 wedges

1 red bell pepper, seeded and cut into strips about ½ inch (12 mm) wide

3 cloves garlic, chopped

2-inch (5-cm) piece of fresh ginger, peeled and chopped

1 can (14 fl oz/430 ml) coconut milk

3 tablespoons red curry paste

1 cup (8 fl oz/250 ml) low-sodium chicken broth

2 tablespoons Asian fish sauce

4 fresh basil leaves, chopped

THAI RED CURRY WITH CHICKEN & SWEET POTATOES

Bring a saucepan of salted water to a boil over high heat. Peel the sweet potatoes and cut them into ½-inch (12-mm) cubes. Add the sweet potatoes and cook until fork-tender, about 6 minutes. Drain well, transfer to a large bowl, and set aside.

Warm 1 tablespoon of the oil in a large, heavy-bottomed saucepan over medium-high heat. Cut the chicken into ½-inch (12-mm) cubes and season all over with salt and pepper. Add it to the hot pan and cook, stirring a few times, until browned on all sides, about 4 minutes total. Using a slotted spoon, transfer to a plate and set aside. Do not wipe the pan clean and keep it over medium-high heat.

Warm the remaining 1 tablespoon oil in the pan and add the onion and bell pepper. Season well with salt and pepper and sauté until the vegetables are soft, about 4 minutes. Stir in the garlic and ginger and cook just until soft, about 2 minutes. Scrape the contents of the pan into the bowl with the sweet potatoes, taking care to get all of the garlic so it doesn't turn bitter. Do not wipe the pan clean.

Open the coconut milk, but do not shake the can. Add the thick cream from the top of the can and the red curry paste to the saucepan and stir to combine. Whisk in the rest of the coconut milk, the broth, and the fish sauce and bring to a simmer over medium-high heat. Return the chicken to the pan and cook until opaque throughout, about 8 minutes. Add the sweet potatoes and other vegetables and cook just until warmed through, about 5 minutes longer. Stir in the basil and serve right away.

SERVES 6

CHOOSE YOUR COLOR

Of the three Thai-style curry pastes, red, yellow, and green, red is the spiciest. Feel free to switch out for yellow or green to reduce the heat factor in this dish. You can also prepare this recipe with just about any protein including tofu, shrimp, or beef, as well as with other vegetables. Serve this over steamed jasmine rice and set out lime wedges for squeezing.

2 tablespoons olive oil

8 chicken drumsticks, about 1½ lb (750 g) total

Kosher salt and freshly ground pepper

½ butternut squash, peeled, seeded, and cut into 1-inch (2.5-cm) cubes (2 cups/10 oz/315 g)

1 red onion, cut into 8 wedges

3 cloves garlic, chopped

⅔ cup (5 fl oz/160 ml) red wine vinegar

½ cup (4 fl oz/125 ml) fresh orange juice

½ cup (4 fl oz/125 ml) low-sodium chicken broth

2 tablespoons pine nuts, toasted

2 tablespoons minced fresh parsley

SWEET & SOUR DRUMSTICKS WITH SQUASH & RED ONIONS

DINNER, ITALIAN-STYLE

This sweet and sour sauce, bursting with the flavors of garlic and tangy orange juice, is called "agrodolce" in Italian cooking. Serve it with rice pilaf, buttered orzo, or warmed Italian bread to soak up all the delicious sauce. When braising chicken, you want to use pieces on the bone so the chicken will remain tender; thighs or breasts also work well with this recipe.

Warm 1 tablespoon of the olive oil in a large, heavy-bottomed saucepan over medium-high heat. Season the drumsticks all over with salt and pepper and add to the hot pan. Cook, turning as needed, until golden brown on all sides, about 8 minutes total. Transfer to a plate and set aside. Do not wipe the pan clean and keep it over medium-high heat.

Warm the remaining 1 tablespoon olive oil in the pan and add the butternut squash and onion. Season well with salt and pepper and cook, stirring often, until the vegetables are soft, about 8 minutes. Stir in the garlic and sauté just until soft, about 1 minute.

Stir in the vinegar and orange juice, scraping up any browned bits on the bottom of the pan. Add the broth and bring to a simmer. Nestle the drumsticks in the sauce, reduce the heat to medium-low, and cover the pan. Simmer gently until the chicken is opaque throughout, about 25 minutes.

Using tongs, transfer the drumsticks to a serving platter. Stir the pine nuts and parsley into the sauce and raise the heat to high. Cook, stirring occasionally, until the sauce thickens, about 5 minutes. Taste and adjust the seasoning. Pour the sauce with the onion and butternut squash over the chicken and serve right away.

SERVES 4–6

WHAT YOU NEED

2 tablespoons olive oil

1 roasting chicken, 4–5 lb (2–2.5 kg),
cut into 8 serving pieces

Kosher salt and freshly ground pepper

2 yellow onions, sliced

1 lb (500 g) brown mushrooms,
brushed clean and thinly sliced

3 cloves garlic, chopped

2 tablespoons Hungarian sweet paprika

1 tablespoon smoked paprika

1½ cups (12 fl oz/375 ml) low-sodium
chicken broth

1 cup (8 oz/250 g) sour cream

1 tablespoon cornstarch

CHICKEN PAPRIKASH

MAKE IT A MEAL

→≫≫≫≫≫≫≫≫≫

Thickened with sour cream and spiced with Hungarian paprika, the delicious sauce in this dish pairs perfectly served atop buttered egg noodles. Complete the meal with a light green salad, such as Shaved Fennel, Radish & Apple Salad (page 110). Hungarian paprika can vary in color from deep brown to bright red, but generally it offers a sweet red pepper flavor.

Warm the olive oil in a large, heavy-bottomed saucepan over medium-high heat. Season the chicken all over with salt and pepper. Working in batches as needed to avoid crowding, add the chicken to the hot pan, skin side down, and cook, turning once, until golden brown on both sides, about 4 minutes per side. Transfer to a plate and set aside. Do not wipe the pan clean and keep it over medium-high heat.

Add the onions to the pan and sauté until tender, about 8 minutes. Add the mushrooms, season with salt and pepper, and sauté until soft, about 4 minutes. Add the garlic and paprikas and cook, stirring constantly, just until the garlic is soft and the paprika is toasted, about 1 minute. Stir in the broth and bring to a boil.

Return the chicken to the pan and nestle in the sauce. Cover, reduce the heat to medium-low, and simmer until the chicken is opaque throughout (no pink should show when you cut in next to a bone, and the chicken juices should run clear), about 25 minutes. Transfer the chicken to a platter.

In a small bowl, stir together the sour cream and cornstarch. Whisk this mixture into the pan and simmer until the sauce thickens, about 4 minutes. Pour the sauce with the onions and mushrooms over the chicken and serve right away.

SERVES 6

WHAT YOU NEED

½ cup (4 oz/125 g) granulated sugar

¾ cup (6 fl oz/180 ml) low-sodium chicken broth

2 tablespoons Asian fish sauce

2 tablespoons peanut or canola oil

5 boneless, skinless chicken thighs, about 1¾ lb (875 g) total, cut into 1-inch (2.5-cm) cubes

Kosher salt and freshly ground pepper

2 shallots, sliced

1 red bell pepper, seeded and thinly sliced

1-inch (2.5-cm) piece of fresh ginger, peeled and grated

1 serrano chile, seeded and sliced into rings

3 cloves garlic, minced

3 bok choy, quartered

CLAY POT CHICKEN WITH BOK CHOY

Combine the sugar and 2 tablespoons water in a heavy-bottomed saucepan over medium-high heat. Using a wooden spoon, stir constantly until the sugar dissolves. Then stop stirring and cook, swirling the pan every few minutes, until the sugar turns a deep amber brown, about 10 minutes. Remove from the heat and carefully add the chicken broth and fish sauce. The mixture will boil up and then settle down. Stir to combine and set the caramel sauce aside.

Warm 1 tablespoon of the oil in a large, heavy-bottomed saucepan over medium-high heat. Season the chicken all over with salt and pepper and add to the hot pan. Cook, stirring occasionally, until light brown on all sides, about 4 minutes. Transfer to a plate and set aside. Do not wipe the pan clean and keep it over medium-high heat.

Warm the remaining 1 tablespoon oil in the pan. Add the shallots and bell pepper and sauté until soft, about 3 minutes. Add the ginger, chile, and garlic and cook just until fragrant and soft, about 30 seconds. Return the chicken to the pan along with all the juices collected on the plate. Stir in the caramel sauce and bring to a boil. Reduce the heat to low, cover, and simmer until the chicken is opaque throughout, about 20 minutes.

While the chicken is cooking, bring a saucepan of salted water to a boil over high heat. Add the bok choy and cook just until tender, about 2 minutes. Drain well and set aside.

Uncover the pan with the chicken, nestle the bok choy in the sauce, and raise the heat to high. Cook just until the sauce thickens a bit, about 5 minutes longer. Serve right away.

SERVES 4

VIETNAMESE TREAT

In this recipe, a few simple ingredients make a boldly flavored dish in which chunks of chicken are cooked in a rich caramel sauce, as they do in Vietnamese cuisine. A traditional clay pot is used in Thai cooking, but we've adapted this recipe to use a basic saucepan. The serrano chile packs a lot of heat, but you can use a milder chile, like a jalapeño, or leave the chile out all together.

WHAT YOU NEED

1 tablespoon olive oil

6 bone-in, skin-on chicken thighs, about 2½ lb (1.25 kg) total

Kosher salt and freshly ground pepper

3 large shallots, sliced

2 cloves garlic, minced

1½ tablespoons fresh rosemary leaves, chopped

1 cup (8 fl oz/250 ml) apple cider

½ cup (4 fl oz/125 ml) low-sodium chicken broth

2 tablespoons cider vinegar

2½ tablespoons unsalted butter

2 Granny Smith apples, peeled, cored, and cut into slices about ½ inch (12 mm) thick

CIDER-BRAISED CHICKEN THIGHS WITH CARAMELIZED APPLES

Warm the olive oil in a heavy-bottomed frying pan over medium-high heat. Season the chicken all over with salt and pepper. Working in batches as needed to avoid crowding, add the chicken to the hot pan, skin side down, and cook, turning once, until golden brown on both sides, about 4 minutes per side. Transfer the chicken to a plate. Do not wipe the pan clean and keep it over medium-high heat.

Add the shallots to the pan and cook, stirring once or twice, until translucent, about 3 minutes. Add the garlic and rosemary and cook just until soft and fragrant, about 1 minute. Stir in the apple cider, broth, and vinegar, scraping up any browned bits on the bottom of the pan. Bring to a boil. Reduce the heat to medium-low. Return the chicken to the pan, skin side up, and nestle it in the sauce. Cover and simmer until the chicken is opaque throughout (no pink should show when you cut in next to a bone, and the chicken juices should run clear), 25–30 minutes.

Using tongs, transfer the chicken to a serving platter and cover with aluminum foil. Raise the heat to high and cook the sauce until nicely thickened, about 10 minutes. Add ½ tablespoon of the butter and stir until melted. Season the sauce with salt and pepper and keep warm over low heat.

Warm the remaining 2 tablespoons butter in a frying pan over medium heat. When the butter is melted and slightly browned, add the apples and sauté until golden brown, flipping them as you stir to cook on both sides, 6–8 minutes.

To serve, pour the sauce over the chicken and mound the apples on top. Serve right away.

SERVES 4–6

BRAISE & DEGLAZE

Braising is a cooking technique that uses moist heat in a covered pot with cooking liquid. You will often see a recipe calling for you to "deglaze the pan and scrape up all the browned bits." Don't skip this important step. The bits contain a lot of flavor that you want to incorporate into the sauce.

1 tablespoon olive oil

1 roasting chicken, 4–5 lb (2–2.5 kg),
cut into 8 serving pieces

Kosher salt and freshly ground pepper

1 yellow onion, chopped

2 cloves garlic, minced

Mix of 2 teaspoons ground cumin, 1 teaspoon
ground coriander, ¼ teaspoon cayenne pepper

1 cinnamon stick

1 can (14½ oz/455 g) diced tomatoes

2 cans (15 oz/470 g each) chickpeas,
rinsed and drained

1 cup (8 fl oz/250 ml) low-sodium chicken broth

½ cup (3 oz/90 g) dried apricots, halved

2 teaspoons cider or sherry vinegar

2 tablespoons chopped fresh cilantro

MOROCCAN CHICKEN WITH CHICKPEAS & DRIED APRICOTS

EXOTIC ONE-POT MEAL

The Mediterranean spice trio
of cumin, coriander, and cinnamon
creates a deep and earthy flavor
in dishes. Loaded with lean
protein and vegetables, this dish
needs only a side of couscous
for soaking up the delicious
sauce, and dinner is complete.

Warm the olive oil in a large, heavy-bottomed saucepan over medium-high heat. Season the chicken all over with salt and pepper. Working in batches as needed to avoid crowding, add the chicken to the hot pan, skin side down, and cook, turning once, until golden brown on both sides, about 4 minutes per side. Transfer to a plate and set aside. Do not wipe the pan clean and keep it over medium-high heat.

Add the onion to the pan, season with salt and pepper, and sauté until translucent, about 5 minutes. Add the garlic and cook just until soft, about 1 minute. Stir in the cumin spice mixture and cinnamon stick and cook until the spices are fragrant and toasted, about 1 minute.

Add the tomatoes with their juices, the chickpeas, and the broth and season with salt and pepper. Bring to a boil, stir in the apricots, and return the chicken to the pan, nestling it in the sauce. Cover, reduce the heat to medium-low, and simmer until the chicken is opaque throughout (no pink should show when you cut in next to a bone, and the chicken juices should run clear), about 25 minutes. Remove and discard the cinnamon stick.

Stir in the vinegar and cilantro. Taste and adjust the seasoning. Serve right away.

SERVES 6

WHAT YOU NEED

½ lb (250 g) sweet Italian sausage,
casings removed

3 tablespoons olive oil

½ yellow onion, chopped

2 ribs celery, chopped

Kosher salt and freshly ground pepper

2 cloves garlic, minced

6 fresh sage leaves, chopped

¼ cup (2 fl oz/60 ml) dry white wine

5 cups (10 oz/315 g) corn-bread cubes
(½-inch/12-mm cubes; about three-fourths of
an 8-inch/20-cm square pan of baked bread)

1 large egg, lightly beaten

1 cup (8 fl oz/250 ml) low-sodium
chicken broth

1 roasting chicken, 5–6 lb (2.5–3 kg)

ROAST CHICKEN WITH CORN BREAD-SAUSAGE STUFFING

Preheat the oven to 425°F (220°C). Warm a nonstick frying pan over medium-high heat. Add the sausage and cook, stirring occasionally and using your spoon to break up any clumps, until the meat is cooked through, about 10 minutes. Using a slotted spoon, transfer to a large bowl. Do not wipe the pan clean, and keep it over medium-high heat.

Warm 1 tablespoon of the olive oil in the pan. Add the onion and celery and season with salt and pepper. Sauté until the vegetables are soft, about 4 minutes. Add the garlic and sage and cook just until soft, about 1 minute. Stir in the wine, bring to a simmer, and cook until the liquid reduces by half, about 2 minutes. Transfer to the bowl with the sausage. Add the corn bread, egg, and broth to the bowl and toss and stir to combine well. Set aside.

Remove the giblets from the chicken and discard (or reserve for another use). Pat the bird dry with paper towels. Brush the outside all over with the remaining 2 tablespoons olive oil and season well inside and out with salt and pepper. Fill the cavity of the chicken with as much of the stuffing as possible. Place the chicken, breast side up, in a roasting pan or cast-iron skillet. Roast in the oven, basting once with the pan juices about halfway through, until the center of the stuffing and the thickest part of a thigh away from the bone both register 165°F (74°C) on an instant-read thermometer, about 1½ hours. If the chicken or the stuffing starts to get too brown during cooking, cover with aluminum foil.

Remove the chicken from the oven, cover loosely with aluminum foil, and let rest for 10–15 minutes. Transfer the stuffing from the chicken to a serving dish. Carve the chicken, arrange on a platter, and serve right away.

SERVES 4–6

CRISP & FLAVORFUL

For beautifully browned chicken skin, dry both the skin and the inside cavity thoroughly. Be sure the stuffing is completely cool before adding it to the chicken cavity. You can cook any extra stuffing that didn't fit in the bird in a buttered baking dish. Add dried fruit or toasted pecan pieces to the stuffing for variations.

2 tablespoons unsalted butter

2 tablespoons olive oil

8 small bone-in, skin-on chicken thighs, about 2½ lb (1.25 kg) total

Kosher salt and freshly ground pepper

40 cloves garlic, peeled but left whole

¼ cup (2 fl oz/60 ml) dry white wine

¾ cup (6 fl oz/180 ml) low-sodium chicken broth

6 red-skinned potatoes, about ¾ lb (375 g) total, scrubbed but not peeled, quartered

6 fresh thyme sprigs

CHICKEN WITH FORTY CLOVES OF GARLIC & POTATOES

BON APPÉTIT

In this French bistro classic, 40 cloves of garlic roast and infuse flavor into the chicken and sauce. The garlic mellows and sweetens as it cooks, leaving behind a pleasing nutty flavor. Potatoes are cooked alongside the chicken and get seasoned from the chicken juices as they roast. Serve this dish with Rosemary-Roasted Carrots with Brown Sugar (page 106).

Preheat the oven to 350°F (180°C). In a large, heavy-bottomed saucepan over medium-high heat, melt 1 tablespoon of the butter in 1 tablespoon of the olive oil. Season the chicken all over with salt and pepper. Working in batches as needed to avoid crowding, add the chicken to the hot pan, skin side down, and cook, turning once, until golden brown on both sides, about 6 minutes per side. Transfer each batch, skin side up, to a 9-by-13-inch (23-by-33-cm) baking dish as it's finished. Set aside. Do not wipe the pan clean and keep it over medium-high heat.

Add the garlic to the saucepan and cook, stirring often, until lightly browned and beginning to soften, 2–3 minutes. Using a slotted spoon, spread the garlic all over the chicken.

Add the wine to the hot saucepan, scraping up any browned bits on the bottom of the pan, and bring to a simmer. Cook until the liquid reduces by half, about 2 minutes. Add the broth and return to a simmer. Add the remaining 1 tablespoon butter. When the butter has melted, season well with salt and pepper and stir to combine. Carefully pour the sauce all over the chicken and garlic.

In a bowl, toss the potatoes with the remaining 1 tablespoon olive oil and season with salt and pepper. Tuck the potatoes in the baking dish all around the chicken. Scatter the thyme sprigs over the top.

Roast until the potatoes are fork-tender and the chicken is opaque throughout (no pink should show when you cut in next to a bone, and the chicken juices should run clear), 35–40 minutes. Serve right away.

SERVES 6

WHAT YOU NEED

Mix of 1½ tablespoons ground cumin and 2 teaspoons chili powder

Kosher salt and freshly ground pepper

6 boneless, skinless chicken thighs, about 2 lb (1 kg) total

2 teaspoons canola oil

2 tablespoons olive oil

1 tablespoon cider vinegar

2½ cups (3 oz/90 g) shredded romaine lettuce

1 cup (2 oz/60 g) peeled and shredded carrots

2 tablespoons chopped fresh cilantro

1 can (15 oz/470 g) pinto beans

6 flat tostada shells

Avocado spread and fresh salsa (see note)

¾ cup (4 oz/125 g) crumbled queso fresco

CHICKEN TOSTADAS WITH AVOCADO & TANGY SLAW

Preheat the oven to 375°F (190°C).

In a large bowl, stir together the cumin mix and ½ teaspoon salt. Add the chicken, drizzle with the canola oil, and toss to coat the chicken evenly with the oil and the spice mixture. Arrange the chicken on a baking sheet and bake until opaque throughout, about 25 minutes. Remove from the oven and let cool. When cool enough to handle, using your fingers or 2 forks, shred the chicken into bite-sized pieces. Cover with aluminum foil to keep warm and set aside.

To make the tangy slaw, in a large bowl, whisk together the olive oil and vinegar, and season with salt and pepper. Add the lettuce, carrots, and cilantro and toss to mix well and coat thoroughly with the dressing. Taste and adjust the seasoning.

Just before serving, rinse and drain the beans, and warm them in a saucepan over medium-low heat.

To assemble, spread each tostada with some of the avocado spread and top with a spoonful or two of the beans and about ½ cup (1 oz/30 g) of the tangy slaw. Distribute the chicken evenly between the tostadas and scatter the queso fresco on top. Serve right away, passing the salsa at the table.

SERVES 4–6

TOPPINGS GALORE

To make an avocado spread for the first layer of the tostada, halve and pit 2 ripe avocados. In a small bowl, mash the avocados with 2 teaspoons fresh lime juice and season with salt and pepper. Serve the tostadas with fresh salsa.

WHAT YOU NEED

1½ tablespoons olive oil

6 bone-in, skin-on chicken thighs, about 2½ lb (1.25 kg) total

Kosher salt and freshly ground pepper

½ cup (4 fl oz/125 ml) low-sodium chicken broth

1 cup (6 oz/185 g) cherry tomatoes, halved

¾ cup (4 oz/125 g) Spanish olives, pitted

3 cloves garlic, halved lengthwise

2 tablespoons fresh oregano leaves

½ cup (2½ oz/75 g) crumbled feta cheese

ROAST CHICKEN THIGHS WITH TOMATOES, OLIVES & FETA

RUSTIC STAPLE

Bursting with the Mediterranean flavors of fresh oregano, salty feta, tart green olives, and roasted tomatoes, this dish is a versatile one. On weeknights, serve with sautéed spinach; for a dinner party, offer a loaf of French bread, high-quality butter, and a frisée salad.

Preheat the oven to 375°F (190°C).

Warm 1 tablespoon of the olive oil in a large frying pan over medium-high heat. Season the chicken all over with salt and pepper. Working in batches as needed to avoid crowding, add the chicken to the hot pan, skin side down, and cook, turning once, until golden brown on both sides, about 4 minutes per side. Transfer each batch, skin side up, to a baking dish as it's finished. Set aside. Do not wipe the pan clean and keep it over high heat.

Add the broth to the hot pan, scraping up any browned bits on the bottom of the pan. Bring to a simmer, then remove from the heat and carefully pour the pan sauce over the chicken in the baking dish.

In a bowl, drizzle the cherry tomatoes with the remaining ½ tablespoon olive oil, season with salt and pepper, and toss to coat. Scatter the tomatoes, olives, garlic, and oregano all over the chicken and around the dish.

Roast until the chicken is opaque throughout (no pink should show when you cut in next to a bone, and the chicken juices should run clear), about 40 minutes. Remove from the oven, sprinkle the feta all over, and return to the oven until the cheese lightly melts, about 5 minutes longer. Serve right away.

SERVES 4–6

4 boneless, skinless chicken breasts,
about 2 lb (1 kg) total

Kosher salt and freshly ground pepper

8 thin slices prosciutto

8 thin slices Gruyère cheese

16 fresh basil leaves

1 tablespoon unsalted butter

1 tablespoon olive oil

CHICKEN ROULADES WITH PROSCIUTTO, GRUYÈRE & BASIL

SERVING TIP

"Roulades" is a serving style that refers to a stuffed and rolled cut of meat. Here thinly pounded chicken breasts are rolled up with salty prosciutto, nutty Gruyère, and fragrant basil. Slicing into the roulades creates beautiful multi-colored pinwheels, that are wonderful served over a bed of sautéed spinach or orzo, or alongside a mixture of grilled or roasted vegetables, such as red peppers, zucchini, and corn.

Preheat the oven to 450°F (230°C).

Cut each chicken breast in half through the thickness (as if you were going to open it like a book, but don't cut all the way through). Working with 1 breast at a time, place the chicken between 2 pieces of plastic wrap and pound with the flat side of a meat pounder to a thickness of about ¼ inch (6 mm). Season both sides with salt and pepper.

Place 1 chicken breast on a work surface, cut side up. Leaving a ½-inch (12-mm) border, top with 2 slices prosciutto, 2 slices Gruyère, and 4 basil leaves. Roll the chicken up tightly lengthwise and tie with kitchen twine in 3 evenly spaced spots. Repeat with remaining chicken breasts.

In a large, heavy-bottomed, ovenproof frying pan, melt the butter in the olive oil over medium-high heat. Add the chicken rolls and cook, turning as needed, until browned on all sides, 8–10 minutes total. Transfer the frying pan to the oven and bake until an instant-read thermometer inserted into the center of a roll registers 165°F (74°C), about 10 minutes. Remove from the oven, cover loosely with aluminum foil, and let rest for 5 minutes. Snip the strings and remove carefully. Cut each roll crosswise into 1-inch (2.5-cm) roulades. Serve right away.

SERVES 4

WHAT YOU NEED

1½ cups (6 oz/185 g) plain dried bread crumbs

1 tablespoon kosher salt

1 tablespoon dried oregano

2 teaspoons dried thyme

2 teaspoons garlic powder

1 teaspoon freshly ground black pepper

¼ teaspoon cayenne pepper

8 chicken drumsticks, about 1½ lb (750 g) total

2 tablespoons unsalted butter, melted

SPICY & CRISPY DRUMSTICKS

Preheat the oven to 400°F (200°C). Coat a baking sheet lightly with cooking spray and line with aluminum foil.

Put the bread crumbs in a large zippered plastic bag and add the salt, oregano, thyme, garlic powder, black pepper, and cayenne. Seal the bag and shake until the spice mixture is thoroughly combined.

Brush the drumsticks with the melted butter and add them, 2 at a time, to the bag. Seal the bag and shake until the drumsticks are nicely coated with the seasoned bread crumbs.

Arrange the drumsticks on the prepared pan. (Use your hands to press any leftover bread crumbs onto the drumsticks.) Bake, turning once about halfway through, until the chicken is opaque throughout (no pink should show when you cut in next to a bone, and the chicken juices should run clear), about 40 minutes. Serve right away.

SERVES 4–6

DINNER FAVORITE

Here's a modern version of the 70s classic, Shake 'N Bake©. Fine bread crumbs work best in this recipe because larger crumbs, like panko, won't stick as easily to the shape of a drumstick. To substitute fresh bread crumbs, tear day-old bread into small piece and pulse it in a food processor until very fine crumbs form. Homemade bread crumbs will keep in an airtight container in the freezer for weeks.

1½ cups (12 oz/370 g) plain whole-milk yogurt

1 tablespoon tomato paste

1 tablespoon fresh lemon juice

2 teaspoons garam masala

1 teaspoon ground turmeric

Kosher salt and freshly ground pepper

¼ teaspoon cayenne pepper

3 lb (1.5 kg) whole chicken wings

Zest and juice of 1 lemon

1 tablespoon chopped fresh cilantro

TANDOORI CHICKEN WINGS WITH LEMON-YOGURT SAUCE

In a large bowl, stir together ¾ cup (6 oz/185 g) of the yogurt, the tomato paste, lemon juice, garam masala, turmeric, 1 teaspoon salt, and the cayenne. Using a sharp, heavy knife, separate the chicken wings into drumettes and wings, discarding the wing tip joint. Add the chicken pieces to the bowl and toss to coat well. Cover and let marinate in the refrigerator for 30 minutes.

Preheat the broiler. Coat a baking sheet lightly with cooking spray, line with aluminum foil, and coat again.

Remove the chicken wings from the marinade and arrange on the prepared pan. Slip under the broiler about 6 inches (15 cm) from the heat source and broil for 8 minutes. Remove the pan from the oven, flip the wings over, and broil until the chicken is opaque throughout, about 8 minutes longer. Do not worry if the wings have blackened spots on them (that's the way tandoori is meant to be!).

To make the yogurt sauce, in a bowl, combine the remaining ¾ cup (6 oz/185 g) yogurt, the lemon juice and zest, and cilantro and stir to mix well. Season with salt and pepper.

To serve, transfer the wings to a platter and spoon the yogurt sauce into a serving bowl alongside. Serve right away.

SERVES 4

ROUND IT OUT

These fun-sized chicken wings pack a serious punch of flavor. To round out a meal, serve the chicken with cubed, roasted potatoes (which can be dunked into the yogurt sauce, too) and a green salad. These wings are equally tasty at room temperature, making them a good choice for parties or picnics.

½ cup (5½ fl oz/170 ml) pure maple syrup

¼ cup (2 fl oz/60 ml) low-sodium soy sauce

1½ tablespoons peeled and grated fresh ginger

3 cloves garlic, minced

⅛ teaspoon freshly ground pepper

2 lb (1 kg) chicken drumettes

1–2 teaspoons sesame seeds, toasted

STICKY SESAME DRUMETTES

WARNING: ADDICTIVE

>>>>>>>>>

Make a batch of these and sit back and watch them disappear. Pair them with Sesame Sugar Snap Peas (page 109) and sesame noodles with julienned vegetables, and dinner is served. Reducing the sauce before you brush the drumettes allows it to thicken enough to adhere to the chicken, creating the perfect sweet and sticky coating.

In a large bowl, whisk together the maple syrup, soy sauce, ginger, garlic, and pepper. Add the chicken drumettes to the bowl and toss to coat well. Cover and let marinate in the refrigerator for at least 1 hour and up to overnight, tossing the drumettes a few times in the marinade.

Preheat the oven to 375°F (190°C). Coat a baking sheet lightly with cooking spray, line with aluminum foil, and coat again.

Remove the drumettes from the marinade, reserving the marinade, and arrange them on the prepared pan. Bake for 15 minutes.

Meanwhile, pour the reserved marinade into a small, heavy-bottomed saucepan and place over high heat. Bring to a boil and cook until the liquid is reduced to a syrupy sauce, about 8 minutes.

Remove the drumettes from the oven and brush the tops with the reduced marinade. Flip the drumettes over, brush the second sides with the marinade, and sprinkle with the sesame seeds. Return to the oven and bake until the chicken is opaque throughout (no pink should show when you cut in next to a bone, and the chicken juices should run clear), about 10 minutes longer. Let cool slightly, then serve right away.

SERVES 4

1½ cups (6 oz/185 g) panko bread crumbs

¼ cup (1 oz/30 g) freshly grated Parmesan cheese

2 teaspoons dried oregano

Kosher salt and freshly ground pepper

2 large eggs

4 boneless, skinless chicken breasts, about 2 lb (1 kg) total, cut into 1½-inch (4-cm) chunks

5 tablespoons (3 fl oz/90 ml) honey

5 tablespoons (2½ oz/75 g) Dijon mustard

1½ tablespoons unsalted butter, melted

4/16/2020
v.g.
J & E liked
esp. honey
sauce (used red
pepper
instead
of mustard

PARMESAN CHICKEN NUGGETS WITH DIPPING SAUCES

Preheat the oven to 375°F (190°C). Coat a baking sheet with cooking spray, line with aluminum foil, and coat again.

On a large plate, whisk together the panko, Parmesan, oregano, 2 teaspoons salt, and ¾ teaspoon pepper. Beat the eggs in a large, shallow bowl.

Season the chicken pieces with salt and pepper. Dip each chicken piece in the eggs, then dredge in the seasoned bread crumbs. Place the nuggets on the prepared pan as you work. Bake the nuggets, turning once about halfway through, until the coating is nicely browned and the chicken is opaque throughout, 15–20 minutes.

While the chicken nuggets are baking, make the sauces:

To make the honey-mustard dipping sauce, in a bowl, stir together the honey, mustard, and melted butter and season with salt. Make the ranch dipping sauce, following the recipe at right.

Serve the nuggets hot, with the two dipping sauces on the side.

SERVES 4

RANCH DIP

To make a ranch dipping sauce, stir together ¼ cup (2 fl oz/60 ml) mayonnaise, ¼ cup (2 oz/60 g) sour cream, ~~⅓ cup (3 fl oz/80 ml) buttermilk~~, 1 teaspoon cider vinegar, 1 clove garlic minced, 2 teaspoons each chopped fresh parsley and dill, and 1 teaspoon minced fresh chives. Season with salt and pepper. Serve these nuggets with carrots, celery, and jicama cut into matchsticks to maximize the dipping fun.

made ½
recipe or
½ t. onion
powder +
½ t. garlic
powder

11/9/19
v.8;
baked for 40 min
used boneless
skinless?
chicken
thighs?

WHAT YOU NEED

3 tablespoons balsamic vinegar

2 tablespoons honey

1½ tablespoons dark brown sugar

1 tablespoon chopped fresh rosemary

1 tablespoon olive oil

2 teaspoons Dijon mustard

2 cloves garlic, chopped

8 chicken drumsticks, about 1½ lb (750 g) total

BALSAMIC, HONEY & ROSEMARY DRUMSTICKS

BAKE OR GRILL

>>>>>>>>>>>>

This delicious marinade makes a wonderful sticky coating on the drumsticks, which can be grilled as well as baked. Be sure to grill them over indirect heat so the rosemary doesn't burn. Serve these drumsticks with Cauliflower Purée with Roasted Garlic (page 107).

In a large bowl, whisk together the vinegar, honey, brown sugar, rosemary, olive oil, mustard, and garlic. Add the drumsticks to the bowl and toss to coat well. Cover and let marinate in the refrigerator for at least 1 hour and up to 8 hours, tossing a few times.

Preheat the oven to 375°F (190°C). Coat a baking sheet with cooking spray, line with aluminum foil, and coat again.

Remove the drumsticks from the marinade and arrange on the prepared pan. Bake, turning once about halfway through, until an instant-read thermometer inserted into the meatiest part of a leg away from the bone registers 165°F (74°C), about 40 minutes. Serve right away.

SERVES 4

4 boneless, skinless chicken thighs,
about 2 lb (1 kg) total

1 tablespoon olive oil, plus more for brushing

Kosher salt and freshly ground pepper

1 cup (8 fl oz/250 ml) mayonnaise

1 tablespoon chili sauce such as sambal oelek

1 hard-boiled egg, peeled and finely chopped

1 tablespoon sweet pickle relish

8 slices sourdough or French bread

8 thin slices Swiss cheese

¾ cup (4½ oz/140 g) sauerkraut, drained

CHICKEN REUBEN PANINI

Preheat the oven to 375°F (190°C).

Place the chicken on a baking sheet. Drizzle with the olive oil, season well with salt and pepper, and toss to coat. Bake until opaque throughout, about 20 minutes. Remove from the oven and let cool. When cool enough to handle, shred the meat into big pieces and set aside.

To make the thousand island dressing, in a bowl, stir together the mayonnaise, chili sauce, egg, and pickle relish. Season well with salt and pepper and refrigerate until ready to use.

To assemble the reubens, brush a slice of bread with olive oil and season with salt and pepper. Place on a work surface, oiled side down. Spread the top with about 1 tablespoon of the Thousand Island Dressing. Layer on the sandwich ingredients in this order: 1 slice of cheese, one-fourth of the chicken, 3 tablespoons of sauerkraut, and 1 slice of cheese. Spread 1 tablespoon of the dressing on a second slice of bread and place on top, dressing side down. Brush the top of the panini with olive oil and season with salt and pepper. Repeat this process to make 3 more sandwiches.

Preheat a panini press to high. Cook the sandwiches in the press 1 or 2 at a time, or according to the manufacturer's instructions, until nicely grill-marked and the cheese is melted, about 4 minutes. Cut in half and serve right away.

SERVES 4

MAKESHIFT PANINI GRILL

If you don't have a panini press, you can still get the same effect by placing your sandwich on a grill pan and setting a large, heavy lid on top. Grill for 2–3 minutes, then flip the sandwich and replace the lid. The homemade thousand island dressing is worth the effort and leftovers will keep in your refrigerator for up to a week. It makes a great dip for celery or crisp endive leaves.

½ cup (4 oz/125 g) plain whole-milk yogurt

4 teaspoons peeled and grated fresh ginger

4 cloves garlic, minced

2 teaspoons garam masala

Kosher salt and freshly ground pepper

3 boneless, skinless chicken breasts, about 1½ lb (750 g) total

2 tablespoons olive oil

½ yellow onion, thinly sliced

½ teaspoon chili powder

¼ teaspoon paprika

1 can (14½ oz/455 g) chopped tomatoes

2 teaspoons tomato paste

½ cup (4 fl oz/125 ml) heavy cream

¼ cup (1½ oz/45 g) thawed frozen peas

Chopped fresh cilantro for garnish

CHICKEN TIKKA MASALA

SPICE UP DINNER

Tikka masala is a speciality of India featuring chunks of chicken marinated and cooked with yogurt and spices for a dish that is brimming with flavor. Garam masala is a mixture of toasted ground spices that includes turmeric, cinnamon, cumin, and cardamom among others. Serve this dish with steamed basmati rice and warmed naan, an Indian flatbread.

In a large bowl, stir together the yogurt, 2 teaspoons of the ginger, half of the garlic, and 1 teaspoon of the garam masala. Season well with salt and pepper. Add the chicken to the bowl and toss to coat thoroughly. Cover and let marinate in the refrigerator for 30 minutes.

Preheat the broiler. Coat a baking sheet lightly with cooking spray. Remove the chicken from the marinade and arrange in a single layer on the prepared pan. (Discard the marinade.) Slip under the broiler about 3 inches (7.5 cm) from the heat source and broil until the chicken is opaque throughout and has blackened spots in several places, about 8 minutes. Set aside.

Meanwhile, make the masala sauce: In a large saucepan, heat the olive oil over medium-high heat. Add the onion and sauté until translucent, about 5 minutes. Add the remaining 2 teaspoons ginger and the remaining garlic and sauté just until soft, about 1 minute. Add the remaining 1 teaspoon garam masala, the chili powder, and paprika, and season with salt and pepper. Cook, stirring constantly, just long enough to toast the spices, about 1 minute. Add the tomatoes with their juices, tomato paste, and cream and bring to a simmer, stirring to mix well. Add the chicken and peas, nestle them in the sauce, and return to a simmer. Cook gently just until the chicken and peas are warmed through, about 5 minutes. Taste and adjust the seasoning with salt and pepper. Garnish with cilantro. Serve right away.

SERVES 4–6

WHAT YOU NEED

6 small boneless, skin-on chicken breast halves, about 2½ lb (1.25 kg) total

5 tablespoons (3 fl oz/80 ml) olive oil

2 teaspoons chopped fresh oregano

Zest and juice of 1 lemon

Kosher salt and freshly ground pepper

1¼ cups (6½ oz/200 g) crumbled feta cheese

5 tablespoons (1½ oz/45 g) pine nuts, toasted

3 green onions, white and tender green parts only, chopped

2 tablespoons dried currants

GRILLED CHICKEN BREASTS WITH FETA & PINE NUT RELISH

Build a medium-hot fire in a charcoal grill or preheat a gas grill to medium-high. Scrape the grill rack clean and coat with cooking spray.

In a large, nonreactive bowl, toss the chicken with 2 tablespoons of the olive oil, 1 teaspoon of the oregano, and the lemon juice. Season well with salt and pepper. Let stand at room temperature for 10 minutes.

In a small bowl, toss together the feta, pine nuts, green onions, currants, the remaining 1 teaspoon oregano, and the lemon zest. Stir in the remaining 3 tablespoons olive oil and season with salt and pepper. Let stand at room temperature while you grill the chicken.

Arrange the chicken, skin side down, directly over the heat. Close the lid on the grill and cook, turning once, until the chicken is opaque throughout, about 6 minutes per side.

Transfer the chicken breasts to a cutting board and cut each across the grain and on the diagonal into ¾-inch (2-cm) slices. While the chicken is still piping hot, top each chicken breast with a generous serving of the relish and serve right away on a platter or the cutting board.

SERVES 4

WARM & COMFORTING

To ensure the cheese relish melts slightly, warm it to room temperature before topping the hot-off-the-grill chicken. Try this relish on baked potatoes, as an omelet filling, or over grilled asparagus and portobello mushrooms. Serve this dish with Quinoa with Dried Apricots, Pistachios & Arugula (page 103) and a glass of rosé wine or pink lemonade.

2 tablespoons red miso paste

3 tablespoons low-sodium soy sauce

3 tablespoons canola or vegetable oil

1 teaspoon toasted sesame oil

Juice of 1 lime

3 cloves garlic, chopped

½ teaspoon granulated sugar

¼ teaspoon red pepper flakes (optional)

6 boneless, skinless chicken thighs, about 2 lb (1 kg) total

16 wooden skewers (7 inches/18 cm or longer), soaked in water for at least 1 hour

RED MISO CHICKEN SKEWERS

MAKE IT A RICE BOWL

→➤➤➤➤➤➤➤➤➤

Turn this dish into a rice bowl by serving the chicken, removed from the skewers, over Toasted Coconut–Green Onion Jasmine Rice (page 115), topped with grilled vegetables, such as asparagus, bok choy, and shiitake mushrooms. Miso is a Japanese fermented seasoning ingredient that imparts an earthy saltiness to the marinade. You can also mix it with olive oil and use it as a glaze on grilled vegetables.

In a large, nonreactive bowl, whisk together the miso paste, soy sauce, canola oil, sesame oil, lime juice, garlic, sugar, and red pepper flakes, if using.

Cut each chicken thigh crosswise into 8 thin strips. Add the chicken to the bowl and toss to coat well. Cover and let marinate in the refrigerator for at least 1 hour and up to 4 hours.

Build a medium-hot fire in a charcoal grill or preheat a gas grill to medium-high.

Drain the skewers and thread each, lengthwise and accordion style, with 3 pieces of chicken. Arrange the skewers on the grill directly over the heat and cook, turning once, until the chicken is opaque throughout, 3–4 minutes per side. Serve right away.

SERVES 4

1 cup (10 oz/315 g) apricot jam

2 tablespoons Sriracha sauce, plus more to taste

2 tablespoons rice vinegar

1 tablespoon low-sodium soy sauce

1 tablespoon Asian fish sauce

1 bunch green onions, trimmed

8 chicken drumsticks, about 1½ lb (750 g) total

2 tablespoons olive oil

Kosher salt and freshly ground pepper

APRICOT-SRIRACHA DRUMSTICKS WITH GRILLED GREEN ONIONS

Build a medium-hot fire in a charcoal grill or preheat a gas grill to medium-high. Scrape the grill rack clean and coat with cooking spray.

In a small bowl, stir together the jam, Sriracha, rice vinegar, soy sauce, and fish sauce. Slice one of the green onions and stir it into the sauce. Set aside at room temperature.

On a baking sheet, drizzle the drumsticks with 1 tablespoon of the olive oil, season well with salt and pepper, and toss to coat.

Arrange the drumsticks on the rack and grill, turning every 6–8 minutes, until the chicken is golden on all sides and an instant-read thermometer inserted into the meatiest part of a leg away from the bone registers 165°F (74°C), about 30 minutes. During the last 10 minutes, brush the chicken generously with the jam sauce. Repeat several times, using all of the sauce. Transfer the drumsticks to a serving platter.

In a bowl, toss the whole green onions with the remaining 1 tablespoon olive oil and season with salt and pepper. Lay the onions on the grill and cook until nicely grill-marked on the first side (lift one to peek), about 2 minutes. Turn the onions and cook for 1 minute longer. Transfer to the platter with the chicken and serve right away.

SERVES 4–6

FOUR-FLAVOR DELIGHT

The glaze for these crowd-pleasing drumsticks uses a combination of sweet, spicy, sour, and salty ingredients for a taste the whole family will love. Grilled green onions add a pretty pop of color to your presentation and the onion flavor is mellowed by the grill. Serve this dish with white or brown rice for a quick weeknight meal.

(handwritten notes: 11/11/15 Y v.g. yum)

WHAT YOU NEED

1 tablespoon peeled and chopped fresh ginger

2 cloves garlic, chopped

½ cup (6 fl oz/185 ml) honey

3 tablespoons low-sodium soy sauce

1 tablespoon rice vinegar

6 bone-in, skin-on chicken thighs, about 2½ lb (1.25 kg) total

(handwritten: used 1.5 lb boneless skinless thighs)

TERIYAKI CHICKEN THIGHS

A FUN CLASSIC

>>>>>>>>>>

Loved by kids and adults alike, classic teriyaki-glazed chicken is at once sweet, sticky, and savory. For an interactive dinner idea, slice the chicken and serve it with rice, sheets of nori, and sliced avocado and let your family make their own sushi wraps.

In a large bowl, whisk together the ginger, garlic, honey, soy sauce, and rice vinegar. Add the chicken and toss to coat well. Cover and let marinate in the refrigerator for at least 1 hour and up to 8 hours.

Build a medium-hot fire in a charcoal grill or preheat a gas grill to medium-high and set it up for both direct and indirect heat: If you are using a charcoal grill, carefully move the hot coals to one side (about half) of the grill. If you are using a gas grill, turn off the middle set of flames when you are ready to grill.

Arrange the chicken thighs, skin side down, on the rack and grill over the indirect heat area (not over the coals) until nicely grill-marked, about 8 minutes. Turn the chicken and move to direct heat (over the coals). Close the lid on the grill and cook until opaque throughout (no pink should show when you cut in next to a bone, and the chicken juices should run clear) or until an instant-read thermometer inserted into the thickest part of a thigh away from the bone registers 165°F (74°C), about 8 minutes longer.

Serve right away. *(handwritten: grilled 4-5 min a side)*

SERVES 4–6

---

1 roasting chicken, 5–6 lb (2.5–3 kg)

2 tablespoons olive oil

3 tablespoons dark brown sugar

2 tablespoons paprika

1 tablespoon chili powder

2 teaspoons onion powder

2 teaspoons kosher salt

1 teaspoon freshly ground pepper

1 can (12 fl oz/375 ml) beer

BEER CAN CHICKEN

Build a medium-hot fire in a charcoal grill or preheat a gas grill to medium-high and set it up for indirect heat: If you are using a charcoal grill, carefully move the hot coals to the outside edges of the grill. If you are using a gas grill, turn off the middle set of flames when you are ready to grill.

Remove the giblets from the chicken and discard (or reserve for another use). Dry the chicken thoroughly with paper towels. Brush the chicken with the olive oil. In a small bowl, stir together the brown sugar, paprika, chili powder, onion powder, salt, and pepper. Using your hands, rub the spice mixture all over the bird.

Empty (or drink!) half of the can of beer. When the grill is hot, place the beer can on the grill, with the open end of the can facing up, over the indirect heat area (not over the coals). Holding the legs of the chicken, slide the body cavity over the can, balancing the bird on the can and using the legs like a tripod. Close the lid on the grill and cook until an instant-read thermometer inserted into the thickest part of a thigh away from the bone registers 165°F (74°C), 1–1¼ hours.

Place a large metal spatula under the beer can and use a hot pad or tongs to hold the chicken, and carefully remove the chicken, with the beer can, from the grill. Let the chicken rest for 10 minutes, then carefully transfer the bird from the beer can to a cutting board. Carve the chicken, arrange on a platter, and serve right away.

SERVES 4–6

PUT A CAN IN IT

The concept behind grilling a whole chicken over a can of beer is that it keeps flavor and moisture circulating in the covered grill throughout the cooking time to give you a juicy, well-seasoned chicken. Use whatever type of beer you like and have on hand and have fun testing different types. If you want to try this technique with a nonalcoholic ingredient, try a can of chicken broth.

1 cup (1 oz/30 g) loosely packed fresh parsley leaves, plus 2 tablespoons chopped

¼ cup (⅓ oz/10 g) loosely packed fresh basil leaves

10 fresh mint leaves

2 cloves garlic, chopped

1 tablespoon Dijon mustard

1 tablespoon capers, rinsed and drained

2 anchovy fillets, drained

Zest and juice of 1 lemon

5 tablespoons (3 fl oz/80 ml) olive oil, plus more as needed

Kosher salt and freshly ground pepper

3 boneless, skinless chicken breasts, about 1½ lb (750 g) total, cut into ¾-inch (2-cm) cubes

3 zucchini, trimmed and cut into ½-inch (12-mm) dice

CHICKEN & ZUCCHINI SPIEDINI WITH SALSA VERDE

GRILL ON A WEEKNIGHT

Spiedini is the Italian version of a kebab. In this recipe, most of the prep work can be done in advance: The spiedini can be skewered, covered tightly, and refrigerated overnight. The salsa can be made a few hours in advance, covered, and set aside at room temperature. Salsa verde is also delicious served with grilled beef and poached salmon. Serve this with Barley with Asparagus & Herbs (page 118).

Soak 15 wooden skewers (7 inches/18 cm or longer) in water for at least 1 hour.

To make the salsa verde, combine the 1 cup (1 oz/30 g) parsley, the basil, mint, garlic, mustard, capers, and anchovies in a food processor. Pulse until the mixture is uniformly finely chopped, using a spatula to scrape down the sides of the bowl as needed. With the motor running, drizzle in 1 tablespoon of the lemon juice and 2 tablespoons of the olive oil. The salsa should be thick, but if you'd like a slightly thinner consistency, add more olive oil. Season with salt and pepper and set aside at room temperature.

Build a medium-hot fire in a charcoal grill or preheat a gas grill to medium-high. In a large, nonreactive bowl, toss the chicken and zucchini with the remaining 3 tablespoons olive oil, lemon zest and remaining lemon juice, and the 2 tablespoons parsley. Season well with salt and pepper. Let stand at room temperature for 10 minutes.

Drain the skewers and thread each with alternating chicken and zucchini pieces, laying the assembled spiedini on a baking sheet as you work. Season again all over with salt and pepper. Working in batches as needed to avoid crowding, grill the spiedini, turning once, until the chicken is opaque throughout, 4–5 minutes per side.

To serve, transfer the spiedini to a serving platter and top with the salsa verde. Serve right away.

SERVES 4–6

WHAT YOU NEED

1 red bell pepper, seeded and roughly chopped

3 serrano chiles, seeded and roughly chopped

3 cloves garlic, roughly chopped

½ cup (¾ oz/20 g) loosely packed fresh cilantro leaves

½ cup (¾ oz/20 g) loosely packed fresh parsley leaves

Zest and juice of 2 lemons

2 teaspoons paprika

1 teaspoon kosher salt

¼ cup (2 fl oz/60 ml) olive oil

1 butterflied chicken, 4–5 lb (2–2.5 kg)

GRILLED PIRI PIRI CHICKEN

In a food processor, combine the bell pepper, chiles, garlic, cilantro, parsley, lemon zest and juice, paprika, and salt. Pulse until the mixture is uniformly chopped, using a spatula to scrape down the sides of the bowl as needed. With the motor running, slowly drizzle in the olive oil and process just until well combined.

Put the chicken, breast side up, in a large glass baking dish and pour the piri piri sauce all over the bird, reserving about ½ cup (4 oz/125 g) for basting while grilling. Using your hands, rub the chicken with the sauce to make sure all surfaces are well coated. Cover and let marinate in the refrigerator for at least 1 hour and up to overnight.

Build a medium-hot fire in a charcoal grill or preheat a gas grill to medium-high and set it up for indirect heat: If using a charcoal grill, carefully move the hot coals to the outside edges of the grill. If you are using a gas grill, turn off the middle set of flames when you are ready to grill.

Place the chicken, skin side down, over the indirect heat area (not over the coals). Close the lid on the grill and cook for 15 minutes. Using tongs or a large metal spatula, turn the chicken. Close the lid and cook for 20 minutes longer. Baste the chicken generously with about half of the reserved piri piri sauce. Turn the chicken again, close the lid, and cook for 5 minutes longer. Generously baste the chicken with the reserved piri piri sauce one more time, flip once more, and cook, with the lid closed, until an instant-read thermometer inserted into the thickest part of a thigh away from the bone registers 165°F (74°C), 5–10 minutes longer. Transfer to a cutting board. Cut the chicken into pieces, arrange on a platter, and serve right away.

SERVES 4–6

v. g.

made sauce for
2 lb. of
skinless boneless
chicken
thighs +
grilled

FLAVOR BOOSTER

Piri piri is a popular Portuguese spicy and sweet sauce made from chiles and fresh herbs. Here it adds beautiful color and flavor to grilled chicken. Butterflying (also known as spatchcocking) chicken means the whole bird is split by removing the backbone and flattening the bird (ask your butcher to do it). This exposes more of the skin to the heat, creating a crispier and juicier bird. Serve with crusty bread for soaking up the sauce.

served sauce with chicken (not used as basting)

5 tablespoons (3 fl oz/80 ml) olive oil

6 thin slices sourdough bread

Kosher salt and freshly ground pepper

1 yellow onion, halved and thickly sliced

8 oz (250 g) white or brown mushrooms, brushed clean and thinly sliced

3 boneless, skinless chicken breasts, about 1½ lb (750 g) total, thinly sliced

1 tablespoon unsalted butter

1 tablespoon all-purpose flour

2 cups (16 fl oz/500 ml) whole milk, warmed

3 oz (90 g) provolone cheese, shredded (about ¾ cup/3 oz/95 g)

4 oz (125 g) Gruyère cheese, shredded (about ½ cup/2 oz/60 g)

2 poblano chiles, roasted and seeded

OPEN-FACE CHICKEN CHEESESTEAKS

NEW TWISTS

→→→→→→→→→

A traditional cheesesteak is made with beef on a soft hoagie bun with melted provolone cheese. This revamped version swaps in chicken for steak and toasted sourdough for the bun. With a heaping addition of mushrooms, onions, poblano chiles, and a creamy cheese sauce made from provolone and Gruyère, this is a hearty meal. If you like, serve these sandwiches with cups of hot tomato soup.

Heat a grill pan over high heat. Using 2 tablespoons of the olive oil, brush each slice of bread on both sides with oil and season with salt and pepper. Place on the pan and cook, turning once, until nicely grill-marked, about 3 minutes per side. Transfer to a plate and set aside. Reduce the heat to medium-high.

In a large bowl, toss the onion and mushrooms with 2 tablespoons of the olive oil and season well with salt and pepper. Place on the pan and cook, turning occasionally, until the vegetables are soft and browned, about 7 minutes. Transfer to a separate plate.

In another large bowl, toss the chicken with the remaining 1 tablespoon olive oil and season well with salt and pepper. Transfer to the pan and cook, turning once or twice, until all the chicken is opaque throughout and nicely browned on both sides, about 8 minutes total. Transfer to the plate with the vegetables and cover to keep warm.

To make the cheese sauce, melt the butter in a saucepan over medium-high heat. Whisk in the flour and cook, blending well, for 1 minute. Slowly add the warm milk and cook, whisking constantly, until the sauce thickens, about 4 minutes. Remove from the heat and add the cheeses, stirring until melted and smooth. Season with salt and pepper.

To assemble, place a slice of grilled bread on each of 6 plates. Top each with a scoop of the chicken, mushrooms, and onion. Cut the chiles lengthwise and top the sandwiches with a few slices. Finish each sandwich with a generous helping of the cheese sauce and freshly ground pepper, and serve right away.

SERVES 4–6

2 tablespoons olive oil

2 teaspoons curry powder

1 teaspoon ground cumin

2 cloves garlic, minced

Juice of ½ lemon

4 boneless, skinless chicken breasts, about 2 lb (1 kg) total, thinly sliced

Kosher salt and freshly ground pepper

Tahini sauce (see note)

1 red onion, halved and cut into ½-inch (12-mm) slices

3 pita breads, halved and carefully split to create 6 pockets

Romaine lettuce leaves, torn to fit inside pitas

2 ripe plum (Roma) tomatoes, thinly sliced

CHICKEN SHAWARMA WITH TAHINI SAUCE

In a bowl, stir together 1 tablespoon of the olive oil, the curry, cumin, garlic, and lemon juice. Add the chicken, season well with salt and pepper, and toss to coat thoroughly. Let stand at room temperature for 20 minutes.

Meanwhile, make the tahini sauce, following the directions at right. In a small bowl, toss the onion with the remaining 1 tablespoon olive oil and season with salt and pepper.

Heat a grill pan or frying pan over high heat or build a medium-hot fire in a charcoal grill or preheat a gas grill to medium-high. When the pan or grill is really hot, add the onion and grill, turning occasionally, until nicely browned all over, about 6 minutes. Transfer to a plate and cover to keep warm. Do not wipe the pan clean.

Add the chicken to the pan or grill and grill, turning once, until opaque throughout and lightly browned on both sides, about 3 minutes per side.

To assemble, carefully fill the pita pockets with the grilled chicken and onion, lettuce leaves, and tomato slices and top with a generous drizzle of the tahini sauce. Serve right away.

SERVES 4–6

EASY SOLUTIONS

To make the tahini sauce, in a bowl, stir together ¾ cup (6 oz/185 g) plain whole-milk yogurt, 1 clove finely minced garlic, 2 tablespoons tahini, 1 tablespoon chopped fresh cilantro, and 1 tablespoon fresh lemon juice, and season with salt and pepper. Serve this dinner with grilled vegetables, such as red peppers, zucchini, and yellow squash. For a gluten-free meal, serve the chicken over a bed of spinach leaves and top with the red onion and tahini sauce.

WHAT YOU NEED

1 roasting chicken, 5–6 lb (2.5–3 kg)

3 tablespoons unsalted butter,
at room temperature

3 lemons

2 tablespoons fresh rosemary leaves, chopped

Kosher salt and freshly ground pepper

2 tablespoons olive oil, plus more as needed

4 cloves garlic, halved lengthwise

½ yellow onion, cut into 3 wedges

LEMON-ROSEMARY ROAST CHICKEN

Preheat the oven to 425°F (220°C).

Remove the giblets from the chicken and discard (or reserve for another use). Dry the chicken thoroughly with paper towels.

In a small bowl, beat the butter with the zest and juice of 1 lemon, the rosemary, and plenty of salt and pepper. Starting at the neck of the chicken, gently loosen the skin from the breasts and the drumsticks. Using your fingers, spread the butter mixture evenly under the skin. Brush the outside of the chicken all over with the olive oil and season well with salt and pepper. Place the chicken, breast side up, in a roasting pan.

Quarter the remaining 2 lemons and toss them in a bowl with the garlic and onion. Season the cavity of the chicken with salt and pepper and fill with the lemons, garlic, and onion, or scatter around the chicken, in the roasting pan, and drizzle in oil.

Roast the chicken in the oven, basting once with the pan juices about halfway through, until an instant-read thermometer inserted into the thickest part of a thigh but away from the bone registers 165°F (74°C), about 1¼ hours.

Remove the chicken from the oven, cover loosely with aluminum foil, and let rest for 15 minutes. Carve the chicken, arrange on a platter, and serve right away.

SERVES 4–6

THE DISH THAT KEEPS GIVING

Here, tart lemon, fragrant rosemary, and a rich mixture of butter and olive oil flavor this delicious chicken. This classic recipe, which requires very little hands-on time, should be added to your weeknight recipe arsenal. What's not eaten for dinner makes fabulous leftovers, whether sliced and eaten cold, or shredded or cubed and reconstituted in chicken salad or enchiladas.

4 tablespoons olive oil

1 small yellow onion, finely chopped

2 cloves garlic, minced

Kosher salt and freshly ground pepper

1¼ cups (10 oz/315 g) ketchup

¾ cup (7½ oz/235 g) orange marmalade

¾ cup (2 fl oz/60 ml) fresh lemon juice

2 tablespoons spicy brown mustard

Hot-pepper sauce, as needed

2 roasting chickens, about 4 lb (2 kg) each, patted dry and cut into 8 serving pieces

BARBECUED CHICKEN WITH SWEET-AND-TANGY SAUCE

SUMMERTIME FAVORITE

Grilled corn on the cob and corn bread are classic accompaniments to this summertime favorite. Serve on a hot day with your favorite beer or tall glasses of cool lemonade. The barbecue sauce can be prepared up to 3 days ahead, cooled, covered, and refrigerated.

To make the sauce, warm 2 tablespoons of the olive oil in a heavy saucepan over medium heat. Add the onion and cook, stirring often, until golden, about 8 minutes. Add the garlic and ½ teaspoon salt and cook, stirring, until fragrant, about 1 minute. Stir in the ketchup, marmalade, lemon juice, and mustard and bring to a low boil. Reduce the heat to medium-low and simmer, stirring often, until slightly reduced, about 20 minutes. Season with hot-pepper sauce to taste. Set aside to cool completely.

Build a medium-hot fire in a charcoal grill or preheat a gas grill to medium-high and set it up for indirect heat: If using a charcoal grill, carefully move the hot coals to the outside edges of the grill. If you are using a gas grill, turn off the middle set of flames when you are ready to grill.

Cut the chicken into 8 parts, separating the drumsticks and the thighs and cutting each breast crosswise into 2 pieces. Brush each piece with the remaining 2 tablespoons olive oil and season with salt and pepper.

Lightly oil the grill rack. Place the chicken, skin side down, over indirect heat and cover the grill. Cook for 20 minutes, turning once. Brush the chicken generously with the sauce and turn again. Cover and cook, turning every 5 minutes and brushing both sides of the chicken with the sauce with each turn, until the chicken reaches an internal temperature of 165°F (74°C), about 15 minutes longer. Serve right away.

SERVES 6–8

4 boneless, skinless chicken breasts, about 1 lb (500 g) total

6 tablespoons (3 oz/90 g) unsalted butter, at room temperature

2 tablespoons olive oil

Kosher salt and freshly ground pepper

Hot-pepper sauce, ½ cup (4 fl oz/125 ml)

2 teaspoons garlic powder

2 teaspoons chopped fresh parsley

2 teaspoons chopped fresh chives

8 slices rustic bread, such as Pugliese or sourdough, each about ½ inch (12 mm) thick

6 oz (185 g) pepper jack cheese, thinly sliced

BUFFALO CHICKEN PANINI

Cut each chicken breast in half through the thickness (as if you were going to open it like a book, but cut all the way through). Working with 1 half at a time, place the chicken between 2 pieces of plastic wrap and pound with the flat side of a meat pounder to a thickness of about ¼ inch (6 mm).

Heat a grill pan over high heat. Meanwhile, melt 2 tablespoons of the butter. Brush both sides of the chicken with the olive oil and season with salt and pepper. Place the chicken on the pan, and cook until nicely grill-marked, about 4 minutes. Flip the chicken and cook until opaque throughout, about 3 minutes longer. Transfer the chicken to a large bowl and add the hot-pepper sauce and the melted butter, tossing a few times to completely cover, and let sit. Keep the pan over high heat.

In a small bowl, stir together the remaining 4 tablespoons (2 oz/60 g) butter, the garlic powder, parsley, and chives, and season with salt and pepper. Spread both sides of each bread slice with the flavored butter and add a slice of cheese on 4 of the bread slices. Remove the chicken from the bowl, letting any excess sauce drip into the bowl and place a piece of chicken on 4 of the bread slices. Top with the remaining cheese, dividing it evenly. Place the remaining 4 bread slices on top.

Place the panini on the grill pan. Place a heavy pot or pan on the top of the panini to act as a lid. Cook until the bread is golden and toasted, the chicken is warmed, and the cheese is melted, flipping halfway through the cooking time, 3–4 minutes total. Serve right away.

SERVES 4

COOL-DOWN DIP

This indulgent sandwich is buttery and spicy. Save any excess sauce as a dip for the panini. Or, if you'd prefer a cooling blue cheese dip, mix together cooling blue cheese dip, mix together 2 parts sour cream, or a mixture of half sour cream and half plain full-fat Greek yogurt, with 1 part crumbled blue cheese. Add a small handful of chopped green onions or chives and season with salt and pepper. Refrigerate or use right away as a dip for your panini.

3 tablespoons unsalted butter

1 tablespoon olive oil

½ yellow onion, chopped

2 carrots, peeled and chopped

2 cloves garlic, minced

6 white or brown mushrooms, brushed and sliced

5 fresh sage leaves, chopped

Kosher salt and freshly ground pepper

½ cup (2½ oz/75 g) thawed frozen peas

¼ cup (1½ oz/45 g) all-purpose flour

1½ cups (12 fl oz/375 ml) low-sodium chicken broth

½ cup (4 fl oz/125 ml) *each* dry white wine and half-and-half

4 cups (1½ lb/750 g) cooked cubed chicken

Purchased or homemade pie dough, refrigerated

CHICKEN POTPIE

QUICK COMFORT FOOD

A creamy mixture of tender vegetables and chicken is blanketed with a flaky pastry dough crust, creating an endlessly comforting dish. This recipe uses store-bought pie dough and the meat from a cooked chicken to help bring this tempting dish to the table even faster. For a glossy finish, brush 1 large egg yolk, beaten with 1 teaspoon water, over the tops of the pies before baking.

Preheat the oven to 375°F (190°C).

In a large frying pan over medium-high heat, warm 1 tablespoon of the butter and the olive oil. Add the onion and the carrots and sauté until soft, about 8 minutes. Add the garlic, mushrooms, and sage and season well with salt and pepper. Cook, stirring occasionally, until the mushrooms are soft, about 4 minutes. Transfer to a large bowl and stir in the peas. Do not wipe the pan clean and keep it over medium-high heat.

Melt the remaining 2 tablespoons butter. Sprinkle in the flour and cook, stirring constantly, for 1 minute. Stir in the broth, wine, and half-and-half and bring to a simmer. Cook, stirring often, until the sauce thickens, about 5 minutes. Remove from the heat, add the cooked chicken and let cool slightly, then add to the bowl with the vegetables and stir to combine well. Season with salt and pepper and divide the mixture among six 4½-inch (11.5-cm) baking dishes.

Remove the dough from the refrigerator, unwrap, and let stand for a few minutes to soften slightly. Roll into a round. Using the bottom of one of the baking dishes as a guide, and with the tip of a sharp knife, cut out 6 circles that are about ¼ inch (6 mm) bigger than the dish. Place the dough over the filling in each dish, pressing the dough onto the rim of the dishes. Crimp the edges and place the dishes on a baking sheet. Bake until the crust is golden brown, 20–25 minutes. Remove from the oven and let cool for 5 minutes. Serve right away.

SERVES 6

4 cups (32 fl oz/1 l) buttermilk

⅓ cup (3 oz/85 g) kosher salt

2 teaspoons *each* dried oregano, thyme, rosemary, and sage

1 teaspoon granulated garlic

½ teaspoon cayenne pepper

1 roasting chicken (about 4½ lb/ 2.25 kg), cut into 8 serving pieces

Canola oil for deep-frying

1⅓ cups (7 oz/215 g) all-purpose flour

1 teaspoon baking powder

½ teaspoon freshly ground black pepper

BUTTERMILK FRIED CHICKEN

To make the buttermilk brine, in a large bowl, whisk together the buttermilk and salt. In a mortar, crush together the oregano, thyme, rosemary, and sage with a pestle (or pulse in a spice grinder) until finely ground. Whisk the ground herbs, garlic, and cayenne pepper into the buttermilk mixture. Cut each chicken breast half crosswise to make 4 breast portions, for a total of 10 chicken pieces. Add to the buttermilk brine, making sure that the chicken is submerged. (If it isn't, transfer everything to a smaller bowl.) Cover and refrigerate for at least 4 hours and up to 6 hours.

Pour oil into a large, heavy saucepan to a depth of at least 3 inches (7.5 cm) and heat to 350°F (180°C) on a deep-frying thermometer. (If you don't have a thermometer, your best test is to dip the edge of a tortilla or bread slice into the oil; it should sizzle immediately and vigorously.) Set a large wire rack on a rimmed baking sheet and place near the stove. Have ready a second rimmed baking sheet. In a large bowl, whisk together the flour, baking powder, and black pepper. Remove half of the chicken from the buttermilk brine, letting the excess brine drip back into the bowl. Add the chicken to the flour mixture and toss to coat evenly, then transfer to the second baking sheet.

When the oil is ready, working in batches to avoid crowding, carefully slip the chicken pieces into the hot oil. The temperature will drop, but adjust the heat to keep the oil bubbling steadily at about 325°F (165°C). Deep-fry the chicken pieces, turning them occasionally with tongs, until they are golden brown and show no sign of pink when pierced at the thickest part, about 12 minutes. Using a wire skimmer, transfer the chicken to the rack to drain. Repeat with the remaining chicken. Serve warm.

SERVES 4–6

CLASSIC COMFORT

A big platter of this crisp, tender, golden brown chicken would be a hit at any potluck or picnic. Immersing the chicken pieces in the buttermilk brine for several hours gives the chicken loads of flavor and helps keep the meat moist as it fries. The acid in the buttermilk also helps to tenderize the chicken. For a Southern-inspired meal, serve with Buttermilk Mashed Potatoes (page 116) and braised collard greens.

4 boneless, skinless chicken breasts, about 2 lb (1 kg) total

10 black peppercorns

1 bay leaf

½ yellow onion

Kosher salt and freshly ground pepper

5 tablespoons (3 fl oz/80 ml) mayonnaise

2 teaspoons Dijon mustard

5 tablespoons (1½ oz/45 g) chopped celery

3 tablespoons finely chopped red onion

3 tablespoons chopped fresh tarragon

TARRAGON CHICKEN SALAD

ENDLESS VARIATIONS

Poaching yields succulent chicken and requires little hands-on time. This method makes the best chicken salad because the meat stays moist from cooking to serving. The variations on the dish are endless. Try chicken salad in a pita pocket, on a bed of lettuce, or on a toasted English muffin with melted Gruyère cheese.

In a heavy-bottomed saucepan over high heat, combine the chicken breasts, peppercorns, bay leaf, and yellow onion. Add cold water to cover by 2 inches (5 cm) and stir in 1 teaspoon salt. Bring to a boil, then reduce the heat to medium-low and simmer until the chicken is opaque throughout, 20–25 minutes. Drain and let cool. When cool enough to handle, cut the chicken into small bite-sized pieces.

In a large bowl, stir together the mayonnaise, mustard, celery, red onion, and tarragon. Add the chicken, toss to coat and mix well, and season with salt and pepper. Serve right away or cover and refrigerate for up to 3 days.

SERVES 4–6

CHICKEN SALAD VARIATIONS

CURRIED Stir together the mayonnaise, celery, and red onion with 1 tablespoon curry powder, 2 tablespoons currants, and 5 chopped dried apricots. Toss with the poached chicken and season with salt and pepper.

ASIAN Stir together the mayonnaise with 2 teaspoons sesame oil, 2 tablespoons chopped fresh cilantro, and 2 teaspoons chopped fresh chives. Toss with the poached chicken and season with salt and pepper.

GRAPES & DILL Stir together the mayonnaise, mustard, celery, and red onion with ¾ cup (4½ oz/140 g) halved purple grapes and 2 tablespoons chopped fresh dill. Toss with the poached chicken and season with salt and pepper.

FENNEL & ORANGE Stir together the mayonnaise and red onion with ¼ cup (1 oz/30 g) chopped fennel bulb, the grated zest of 1 orange, and 1 tablespoon fresh orange juice. Toss with the poached chicken and season with salt and pepper.

12 tomatillos, papery husks removed

3 poblano chiles, halved lengthwise and seeded

1½ white onions, chopped

2 cloves garlic, chopped

1½ cups (1½ oz/45 g) loosely packed fresh cilantro leaves, chopped

Kosher salt and freshly ground pepper

2 tablespoons olive oil

1 small red bell pepper, seeded and chopped

1½ tablespoons ground cumin

2 cups (12 oz/375 g) cooked shredded chicken

1 lb (500 g) Monterey jack cheese, shredded

1 can (15 oz/470 g) black beans, rinsed and drained

12 flour tortillas

CHICKEN & BLACK BEAN ENCHILADAS

Preheat the broiler. Rinse the tomatillos under warm water to dissolve the sticky coating on the skins. Pat dry and cut in half. Arrange the tomatillos and chiles, cut side down, on a baking sheet, slip under the broiler, and broil until the skins are charred, about 7 minutes. Let cool for a few minutes. Lower the oven temperature to 350°F (180°C).

Working in batches as needed to avoid crowding the blender jar, combine the tomatillos, chiles, two-thirds of the onions, the garlic, and 1 cup (1 oz/30 g) of the cilantro in a blender and process to a smooth purée. Transfer the tomatillo sauce to a bowl and season with salt and pepper. Set aside.

Warm the olive oil in a frying pan over medium-high heat. Add the remaining onions and the bell pepper and season with salt and pepper. Sauté until the vegetables are soft, about 5 minutes. Stir in the cumin and cook, stirring, just to toast the cumin, about 30 seconds. Transfer to a large bowl and stir in the chicken, about half of the cheese, ¾ cup (6 fl oz/180 ml) of the tomatillo sauce, and the remaining ½ cup (½ oz/15 g) cilantro. Stir the beans into the chicken mixture. Season with salt and pepper.

Spread a few tablespoons of the tomatillo sauce on the bottom of a large baking dish. Fill each tortilla with ⅓ cup (3 oz/90 g) of the chicken mixture, roll up tightly, and place, seam side down, in the baking dish. Cover the enchiladas with the remaining tomatillo sauce and scatter the remaining cheese on top. Cover the baking dish with aluminum foil and bake for 30 minutes. Remove the foil and continue baking until the sauce is bubbling and the cheese is lightly browned, about 10 minutes longer. Serve right away.

SERVES 4–6

FEED A CROWD

Entertaining a large group? Enchiladas are the perfect solution as the recipe can easily be doubled or quadrupled to feed a crowd. The sauce can be made and refrigerated a day in advance, and the enchiladas can be fully prepped and refrigerated up to 1 hour before baking. Top servings with sliced avocado and tomato salsa, if you like.

4 tablespoons (2 fl oz/60 ml) olive oil

8 oz (250 g) white or brown mushrooms, brushed clean and sliced

Kosher salt and freshly ground pepper

10 oz (315 g) spinach leaves, tough stems removed

4 boneless, skinless chicken breasts, about 2 lb (1 kg) total

½ cup (2½ oz/75 g) all-purpose flour

1 cup (4 oz/125 g) plain dried bread crumbs

2 large eggs

3½ cups (28 oz/875 g) prepared marinara sauce

8 oz (250 g) fresh mozzarella cheese, preferably buffalo, thinly sliced

6 tablespoons (1½ oz/45 g) freshly grated Parmesan cheese

CHICKEN PARMESAN WITH SAUTÉED MUSHROOMS & SPINACH

A MODERN CLASSIC

>>>>>>>>>>>

This updated classic includes lots of vegetables making it a nutritious meal all ages will enjoy. Serve with warm bread or buttered spaghetti. Spoon any excess marinara sauce in the bottom of the baking dish and around the chicken breasts to keep the meat moist during cooking. To ensure the bread crumbs stay toasted and don't become soggy, serve this dish right out of the oven.

Preheat the oven to 450°F (230°C). Warm 1 tablespoon of the olive oil in a large frying pan over medium-high heat. Add the mushrooms, season with salt and pepper, and cook, stirring often, until soft, about 4 minutes. Transfer to a plate; do not wipe the pan clean. Warm 1 tablespoon of the olive oil in the same pan and add the spinach. Cook, stirring constantly, until the spinach just begins to wilt, about 2 minutes. Transfer to a separate plate and set aside. Wipe the pan clean and reserve.

Working with 1 chicken breast at a time, place the chicken between 2 pieces of plastic wrap and pound with the flat side of a meat pounder to a thickness of about ¼ inch (6 mm). Pour the flour onto a large plate and season it well with salt and pepper. Pour the bread crumbs onto another plate and season with salt and pepper. Lightly beat the eggs with 1 tablespoon water in a shallow bowl.

In the reserved frying pan, heat the remaining 2 tablespoons olive oil over medium-high heat until very hot but not smoking. Working with 1 at a time, lightly dredge the pounded chicken pieces first in the seasoned flour; then in the egg wash, letting the excess drip off; then in the bread crumbs. When the oil is very hot but not smoking, working in batches as needed to avoid crowding the pan, add the cutlets and fry, turning once, until golden and crusty on both sides, about 4 minutes per side.

Transfer the chicken cutlets as they are finished to a baking dish. Ladle the marinara sauce over the chicken and top with the spinach and mushrooms. Arrange the mozzarella slices on top and sprinkle with the Parmesan. Bake until the chicken is opaque throughout and the cheese is melted, about 15 minutes. Serve right away.

SERVES 4

SIDES & SALADS

2 cups (16 fl oz/500 ml) low-sodium chicken or vegetable broth

1 cup (7 oz/220 g) quinoa

2 tablespoons olive oil, plus more for drizzling

¼ cup (1 oz/30 g) chopped yellow onion

2 cloves garlic, minced

2 cups (2 oz/60 g) loosely packed fresh arugula leaves, tough stems removed

Kosher salt and freshly ground pepper

½ cup (3 oz/90 g) dried apricots, quartered

3 tablespoons pistachios

2 tablespoons chopped fresh parsley

QUINOA WITH DRIED APRICOTS, PISTACHIOS & ARUGULA

Pour the broth in a saucepan and bring to a boil over medium-high heat. Add the quinoa, return to a boil, cover, and reduce the heat to low. Simmer until all the liquid has been absorbed, about 12 minutes. Remove from the heat and let the quinoa stand, covered, for 10 minutes.

Meanwhile, warm the olive oil in a frying pan over medium-high heat. Add the onion and sauté until translucent, about 5 minutes. Add the garlic and sauté just until soft, about 1 minute. Stir in the arugula and cook, stirring occasionally, just until slightly wilted, about 2 minutes. Season with salt and pepper.

Transfer the contents of the frying pan to a large bowl. Stir in the quinoa, apricots, pistachios, and parsley. Drizzle with a little more olive oil. Taste and adjust the seasoning. Serve right away.

SERVES 4–6

SUPERFOOD SIDE DISH

Quinoa, which has high levels of protein and fiber, is versatile and cooks quickly. It's also a healthy way of soaking up delicious sauces. For a balanced meal, serve this with Balsamic, Honey & Rosemary Drumsticks (page 60) and grilled asparagus.

Kosher salt and freshly ground pepper

1 small bunch broccoli rabe,
tough stems removed

4 tablespoons (2 fl oz/60 ml) olive oil

½ yellow onion, chopped

2 cloves garlic, minced

1 can (15 oz/470 g) white beans,
rinsed and drained

Zest and juice of 1 lemon

LEMONY WHITE BEANS WITH BROCCOLI RABE

GO-TO NUTRIENTS

>>>>>>>>

This easy, nutrient-rich side
comes together quickly thanks
to canned beans, a great pantry
staple for weeknight dinners.
You can also serve this dish as
a flavorful topping on slices of
toasted bread. Broccolini or baby
bok choy are good substitutes for
the broccoli rabe.

Bring a saucepan of salted water to a boil over high heat. Add the broccoli rabe and
cook just until the stems are fork-tender, about 4 minutes. Drain well and let cool.
When cool enough to handle, cut into 2-inch (5-cm) pieces and set aside.

Warm 2 tablespoons of the olive oil in a frying pan over medium-high heat. Add the
onion and sauté until soft, 3–4 minutes. Add the garlic and sauté just until soft, about
30 seconds. Stir in the beans and broccoli rabe and season with salt and pepper. Cook,
stirring a few times, until the beans and broccoli rabe are warmed through, 2–3 minutes.

Stir in the lemon zest and juice and the remaining 2 tablespoons olive oil. Taste and
adjust the seasoning. Serve right away.

SERVES 4–6

2 tablespoons unsalted butter,
at room temperature

2 tablespoons dark brown sugar

1 tablespoon fresh rosemary leaves, chopped

½ teaspoon kosher salt

¼ teaspoon chili powder

1 lb (500 g) carrots, peeled, trimmed and
cut into ½-inch (12-mm) pieces or halved
lengthwise

ROSEMARY-ROASTED CARROTS WITH BROWN SUGAR

SPICE IT UP

➤➤➤➤➤➤➤➤

These sweet-scented carrots will tempt you as they roast and your kitchen is filled with a delicious aroma. If some carrots are bigger than others in the bunch, cut them in half lengthwise. You want them to be about the same thickness so they cook evenly. This spice combination also works well on parsnips and sweet potatoes.

Preheat the oven to 400°F (200°C).

In a small bowl, beat together the butter, brown sugar, rosemary, salt, and chili powder. Arrange the carrots in a single layer on a baking sheet. Using your hands, spread the butter mixture all over the carrots.

Roast the carrots, turning once about halfway through, until fork-tender, 25–30 minutes. Serve right away.

SERVES 4

3–5 cloves garlic, unpeeled

1 tablespoon olive oil

Kosher salt and freshly ground pepper

1 head cauliflower, thick stems removed, cut into small florets

4 tablespoons (2 oz/60 g) unsalted butter

½ cup (4 fl oz/125 ml) heavy cream

11/19/19
v.g.
—garlic did not work in toaster oven
—otherwise light purée

CAULIFLOWER PURÉE WITH ROASTED GARLIC

Preheat the oven to 450°F (230°C).

Put the garlic cloves on a sheet of aluminum foil and drizzle with the olive oil. Wrap loosely in the foil and place in the oven. Roast until the garlic is very soft and browned, about 25 minutes. Remove from the oven and let cool.

Bring a saucepan of salted water to a boil over high heat. Add the cauliflower and cook until tender, 8–10 minutes. Drain well and return the cauliflower to the warm pan over high heat. Cook the cauliflower, stirring constantly with a wooden spoon, to get rid of any excess moisture, about 2 minutes. Transfer the cauliflower to a blender or food processor. Squeeze in the roasted garlic, discarding the skins.

Combine the butter and cream in a clean saucepan over medium heat. When the butter has melted and the cream is warm (do not let it boil), pour the mixture into the blender or food processor with the cauliflower. Process to a smooth purée. Season with salt and pepper and serve right away.

SERVES 4–6

HEALTHY ALTERNATIVE

This light purée is a great alternative to mashed potatoes. Serve with Chicken with Forty Cloves of Garlic & Potatoes (page 44)—you can just pluck a few cloves of roasted garlic right out of the roasting pan and you are ready to go for the purée.

1 lb (500 g) sugar snap peas, trimmed and any strings removed

1 teaspoon toasted Asian sesame oil

1 teaspoon sesame seeds, toasted

Kosher salt and freshly ground pepper

SESAME SUGAR SNAP PEAS

Bring a saucepan of salted water to a boil over high heat. Add the snap peas and cook just until they begin to soften, about 2 minutes. Drain well and transfer to a bowl.

Drizzle the sesame oil over the snap peas, sprinkle in the sesame seeds, and toss to coat evenly. Season with salt and pepper and serve right away.

SERVES 4

WEEKNIGHT ARSENAL

Quick, fresh, and healthy, this recipe is ideal for any night of the week, especially in spring and summer when sugar snap peas are at their best. To string a sugar snap pea, snap the tough end and then pull the string the length of the pea. Serve with Red Miso Chicken Skewers (page 68) and Toasted Coconut-Green Onion Jasmine Rice (page 115).

¼ cup (2 fl oz/60 ml) fresh grapefruit juice

1 tablespoon fresh lemon juice

½ teaspoon honey

Kosher salt and freshly ground pepper

2 tablespoons olive oil

1 large fennel bulb

6 radishes

1 apple, preferably Pink Lady, cored and thinly sliced

3 oz (90 g) Parmesan cheese

SHAVED FENNEL, RADISH & APPLE SALAD

KEEP IT LIGHT

>>>>>>>>>

Refreshing and crisp, this citrusy salad is tossed in a tangy grapefruit vinaigrette and is perfect for serving at a barbecue. The acid in the grapefruit and lemon will keep the apple from turning brown, so the salad can sit at room temperature for a few hours. You can use any citrus in the dressing—try blood oranges or Meyer lemons.

To make the vinaigrette, in a small bowl, whisk together the grapefruit juice, lemon juice, and honey. Season with salt and pepper. Drizzle in the olive oil slowly, whisking until well blended. Set aside.

Cut off the feathery tops of the fennel bulb and discard, reserving some fronds for garnish. Core the bulb, cut into quarters, and slice very thinly with a sharp knife or mandoline. Transfer to a large bowl.

Trim the radishes, cut in half, and slice very thinly. Quarter the apple and slice very thinly. Add the radishes and the apple to the bowl with the fennel. Pour the vinaigrette over the salad and toss well to combine. Taste and adjust the seasoning, keeping in mind that the Parmesan will add saltiness.

Transfer the salad to a serving bowl or platter. Using a very sharp knife, cut the Parmesan into small shards. Garnish the salad with the shards and the reserved fennel fronds. Serve right away.

SERVES 4–6

7 cups (7 oz/215 g) mixed salad greens

1 cup (1 oz/30 g) mixed fresh herb leaves, such as tarragon, flat-leaf parsley, dill, chervil, and chives

Extra-virgin olive oil, as needed

Kosher salt and freshly ground pepper

3 teaspoons white wine vinegar

6 oz (180 g) goat cheese, crumbled

HERBED GARDEN SALAD WITH GOAT CHEESE

KEEP IT SIMPLE

→→→→→→→→→→

Fresh and delicious, this is the perfect simple salad to accompany nearly any recipe in this book and beyond. It shows off the bright flavor of fresh greens and fragrant herbs. Mix different kinds of greens; try bitter chicory and radicchio, spicy watercress and arugula, and mild butter lettuce and baby spinach.

In a large bowl, combine the greens and herbs. Drizzle with just enough olive oil to coat lightly and then toss. Season with salt and pepper, and then toss the greens again and taste.

Drizzle with 1–2 teaspoons vinegar and toss. Taste for tanginess and seasoning and adjust with salt, pepper, and vinegar as needed.

Sprinkle the goat cheese over the top and serve right away.

SERVES 6

SALAD VARIATIONS

In spring, add sliced blanched asparagus, diced cooked artichoke hearts, or fava beans with shaved pecorino.

In summer, toss in fresh corn kernels, cherry tomatoes or diced heirloom tomatoes, and cucumber slices.

In fall, add apple, pear, or Fuyu persimmon slices, or pomegranate seeds.

In winter, tangerine, grapefruit, or blood orange sections are good additions. Crushed or whole toasted almonds, pine nuts, or pecans add crunch, while a blue-veined cheese, such as Gorgonzola, or shards of a salty, nutty hard cheese, like pecorino or Parmesan, can replace the goat cheese.

1 large shallot, coarsely chopped

1 tablespoon chopped fresh thyme

1 tablespoon chopped fresh sage

1 tablespoon chopped fresh oregano

1 large clove garlic, coarsely chopped

1 bay leaf, finely crumbled

Kosher salt and freshly ground pepper

½ cup (4 fl oz/125 ml) olive oil

16 red or white new potatoes, about 2 lb (1 kg) total, scrubbed, patted dry, and quartered

ROASTED NEW POTATOES

Preheat the oven to 375°F (190°C). Coat a baking sheet lightly with cooking spray.

In a blender or food processor, combine the shallot, thyme, sage, oregano, garlic, bay leaf, ¼ teaspoon salt, and ½ teaspoon pepper. Add the olive oil and blend just until the shallot is finely chopped. Transfer ⅓ cup (3 fl oz/80 ml) of the herb mixture to a large bowl.

Add the potatoes to the bowl with the herb mixture and toss to coat well. Transfer the potatoes to the prepared baking sheet. Spread out in a single layer and season generously with salt and pepper. Bake the potatoes, turning occasionally for even browning, until tender when pierced with a small knife and golden brown, about 45 minutes. Drizzle with the remaining herb mixture and serve right away.

SERVES 4–6

EASY SEASONING

Here, a fragrant mix of 5 herbs coats crisp oven-roasted potatoes in a blend you'll turn to again and again. This simple preparation produces high-flavor potatoes that pair well with chicken. Chop up any leftovers and add to salads or eggs. You can change up the seasoning with any mixture of your favorite chopped fresh herbs.

1 cup (7 oz/220 g) jasmine rice

½ cup (2 oz/60 g) shredded unsweetened coconut

2 tablespoons canola oil

2 green onions, white and tender green parts only, chopped

1 tablespoon peeled and grated fresh ginger

1 small jalapeño chile, seeded and finely chopped

¼ cup (⅓ oz/10 g) loosely packed fresh cilantro leaves, chopped

Kosher salt and freshly ground pepper

TOASTED COCONUT–GREEN ONION JASMINE RICE

Cook the rice according to package directions. Keep covered in the pan until ready to use.

Preheat the oven to 350°F (180°C).

Spread the coconut in a single layer on a baking sheet. Bake until golden brown, about 4 minutes. Remove from the oven and set aside.

Warm the oil in a frying pan over medium heat. Add the green onions, ginger, and jalapeño and sauté just until the vegetables soften and become fragrant, about 1 minute. Transfer to a bowl. Add the steamed rice, toasted coconut, and cilantro and toss to mix. Season with salt and pepper and serve right away.

SERVES 4

DRESSED-UP RICE

This simple recipe transforms basic steamed rice into an aromatic dish that adds flavor and color to any meal. Serve it alongside a saucy dish, such as Clay Pot Chicken with Bok Choy (page 35). You can also use this combination of fresh elements with other grains, including brown rice, quinoa, farro, and barley.

1½ lb (750 g) Yukon gold potatoes, peeled and cut into 1-inch (2.5-cm) cubes

Kosher salt and freshly ground pepper

4 tablespoons (2 oz/60 g) unsalted butter

½ cup (4 fl oz/125 ml) buttermilk

2 tablespoons chopped fresh chives (optional)

BUTTERMILK MASHED POTATOES

PERFECT POTATOES

There are a few basic rules for creating foolproof mashed potatoes. Starchy (russet) or waxy (Yukon gold) potatoes are best for a creamy mash. Cut the potatoes in a uniform size so they cook evenly. Make sure the butter and buttermilk are warm so they will absorb into the potatoes better. These luscious potatoes are a perfect accompaniment for Chicken Piccata with Artichokes (page 19).

Put the potatoes in a saucepan and add cold water to cover by 2 inches (5 cm). Stir in 1 teaspoon salt and bring to a boil over medium-high heat. Cook until the potatoes are fork-tender, about 15 minutes. Drain well, then return the potatoes to the warm pan. Continue to cook the potatoes over medium heat, stirring often with a wooden spoon, to remove any excess moisture from the potatoes, about 2 minutes more. Set aside.

Melt the butter in a small saucepan over low heat. Add the buttermilk and cook just until warm; do not let it boil.

Using a potato masher or 2 forks, mash the potatoes until smooth. Stir in the warm buttermilk mixture. Fold in the chives, if using. Season with salt and pepper and serve right away.

SERVES 4–6

1 cup (7 oz/220 g) farro

2½ cups (20 fl oz/625 ml) low-sodium chicken broth

¼ cup (2 fl oz/60 ml) olive oil

3 cloves garlic, thinly sliced

4 ripe plum (Roma) tomatoes, chopped

Kosher salt and freshly ground pepper

2 cups (2 oz/60 g) loosely packed fresh spinach leaves, tough stems removed

¼ cup (⅓ oz/10 g) loosely packed fresh basil leaves, chopped

FARRO WITH GARLIC, TOMATOES & BASIL

Combine the farro and broth in a saucepan and bring to a boil over medium-high heat. Reduce the heat to low and simmer, uncovered, until the farro is tender but still a bit crunchy, about 15 minutes. Strain the broth into another saucepan or a heatproof bowl, reserving the farro and the broth separately.

Warm the olive oil in a large frying pan over medium-high heat. Add the garlic and sauté just until soft, about 30 seconds. Add the tomatoes and season with salt and pepper. Cook, stirring occasionally, until the tomatoes begin to release their juices, about 3 minutes.

Stir in the farro and ¼ cup (2 fl oz/60 ml) of the broth. Add the spinach and cook, stirring to combine, just until wilted, about 2 minutes. Stir in the basil and season with salt and pepper. Add the remaining broth by the spoonful as needed if the farro seems dry. Serve right away.

SERVES 4

NUTTY & NUTRITIOUS

Here, farro—a nutty, whole grain—is combined with garlic, tomatoes, and fresh basil for a wholesome side dish. In the winter months, you can substitute chopped broccoli rabe or strips of chard for the tomatoes. This dish pairs well with roasted and grilled chicken, such as Lemon-Rosemary Roast Chicken (page 87) or Chicken & Zucchini Spiedini with Salsa Verde (page 74).

Kosher salt and freshly ground pepper

1 lb (500 g) asparagus, tough woody ends snapped or cut off, cut into 1-inch (2.5-cm) pieces

4 cups (32 fl oz/1 l) low-sodium chicken or vegetable broth

2 tablespoons olive oil

1 small yellow onion, chopped

2 cloves garlic, minced

2 teaspoons chopped fresh thyme

4 fresh sage leaves, chopped

1 cup (7 oz/220 g) pearl barley

½ cup (4 fl oz/125 ml) dry white wine

6 tablespoons (1½ oz/45 g) freshly grated Parmesan cheese, plus more for serving

BARLEY WITH ASPARAGUS & HERBS

RISOTTO-STYLE GRAINS

Here, barley is cooked in the same manner as Arborio rice in risotto—warm liquid is slowly added to toasted grains to create a creamy consistency. Adapt this recipe throughout the year with other vegetables such as delicata squash in the winter, zucchini in the summer, and fava beans or fresh peas in the spring.

Bring a saucepan of salted water to a boil over high heat. Add the asparagus and cook just until tender-crisp, about 2 minutes. Drain, rinse under cold water, and drain again. Set aside.

Warm the broth in a clean saucepan over low heat.

In a large, heavy-bottomed saucepan, warm the olive oil over medium-high heat. Add the onion and sauté until translucent, about 5 minutes. Add the garlic, thyme, and sage and season with salt and pepper. Sauté just until the garlic softens, about 1 minute. Stir in the barley and toast, stirring often, for about 2 minutes. Add the wine and simmer until absorbed, about 2 minutes.

Reduce the heat to medium-low. Using a ladle, add about ½ cup (4 fl oz/125 ml) of the warm broth at a time, stirring often and allowing each addition to be absorbed before adding the next ladleful of broth. This will take about 35 minutes in total.

When all of the broth has been absorbed, stir in the asparagus and the Parmesan and cook until the asparagus is warmed through, about 2 minutes. Taste and adjust the seasoning. Serve right away, passing extra Parmesan at the table.

SERVES 4–6

MENUS

From busy weeknights with the kids to entertaining guests on a Saturday, planning
a delicious, balanced dinner is a cinch with these menus as your guide.

MANIC MONDAY

A quick stir-fry served in nutritious lettuce cups comes
together in minutes. Make it a meal with a side of easy
rice that can be cooked a day in advance.

CHICKEN IN LETTUCE CUPS (page 23)
TOASTED COCONUT–GREEN ONION JASMINE RICE (page 115)
FOR THE KIDS & ADULTS Seltzer with lemon and lime

GRILL NIGHT

Keep it fun and simple with skewered chicken and
vegetables that grill simultaneously.

CHICKEN & ZUCCHINI SPIEDINI WITH SALSA VERDE (page 74)
RED MISO CHICKEN SKEWERS (page 68)
SHAVED FENNEL, RADISH & APPLE SALAD (page 110)
FOR THE ADULTS Your favorite beer
FOR THE KIDS Sparkling lemonade

ROMANTIC NIGHT-IN

An elegant and flavorful chicken dish and perfectly
crafted cocktails are just the ticket for date night.

CHICKEN WITH FORTY CLOVES OF GARLIC & POTATOES (page 44)
LEMONY WHITE BEANS WITH BROCCOLI RABE (page 104)
FOR THE ADULTS Your favorite cocktail

"KID-FRIENDLY"

Kids will have almost as much fun dipping chicken nuggets into
panko before an adult bakes them as they'll enjoy eating them.

PARMESAN CHICKEN NUGGETS WITH DIPPING SAUCES (page 59)
CAULIFLOWER PURÉE WITH ROASTED GARLIC (page 107)
SESAME SUGAR SNAP PEAS (page 109)
FOR THE KIDS & ADULTS Your favorite soda

COMFORT FOOD NIGHT

A juicy roasted chicken and a side of silky mashed potatoes—
that's old-fashioned comfort food for adults and kids alike.

LEMON-ROSEMARY ROAST CHICKEN (page 87)
BUTTERMILK MASHED POTATOES (page 116)
HERBED GARDEN SALAD WITH GOAT CHEESE (page 112)
FOR THE ADULTS Red wine
FOR THE KIDS Root beer

ITALIAN NIGHT

Simple, satisfying Italian fare gets a healthful twist with the
addition of vegetables and whole grains to classic dishes.

**CHICKEN PARMESAN WITH SAUTÉED MUSHROOMS
 & SPINACH** (page 98)
BARLEY WITH ASPARAGUS & HERBS (page 118)
FOR THE ADULTS Your favorite wine

INDEX

weldon**owen**

415 Jackson Street, 3rd Floor, San Francisco, CA 94111
www.weldonowen.com

CHICKEN NIGHT

Conceived and produced by Weldon Owen, Inc.
In collaboration with Williams-Sonoma, Inc.
3250 Van Ness Avenue, San Francisco, CA 94109

A WELDON OWEN PRODUCTION

Copyright © 2014 Weldon Owen, Inc.
and Williams-Sonoma, Inc.

Printed and bound in China by 1010 Printing, Ltd.

First printed in 2014
10 9 8 7 6 5 4 3 2 1

Library of Congress Control Number: 2014943772

ISBN 13: 978-1-61628-798-6
ISBN 10: 1-61628-798-5

Weldon Owen is a division of
BONNIER

WELDON OWEN, INC

CEO and President Terry Newell
VP, Sales and Marketing Amy Kaneko
VP, Publisher Roger Shaw

Associate Publisher Amy Marr
Associate Editor Emma Rudolph

Creative Director Kelly Booth
Senior Production Designer Rachel Lopez Metzger

Production Director Chris Hemesath
Associate Production Director Michelle Duggan

Photographer Erin Kunkel
Food Stylist Erin Quon
Prop Stylist Leigh Noe

ACKNOWLEDGEMENTS

Weldon Owen wishes to thank the following people for
their generous support in producing this book:
Kris Balloun, David Bornfriend, Marisa Kwek, Ashley Lima, Chuck Luter,
Eve Lynch, Lori Nunokawa, Elizabeth Parson, and Sharon Silva